HOW WE READ

Before you start to read this book, take this moment to think about making a donation to punctum books, an independent non-profit press,

@ https://punctumbooks.com/support/

If you're reading the e-book, you can click on the image below to go directly to our donations site. Any amount, no matter the size, is appreciated and will help us to keep our ship of fools afloat. Contributions from dedicated readers will also help us to keep our commons open and to cultivate new work that can't find a welcoming port elsewhere. Our adventure is not possible without your support.

Vive la Open Access.

Fig. 1. Hieronymus Bosch, *Ship of Fools* (1490–1500).

How We Read

Tales, Fury, Nothing, Sound

**Edited by Kaitlin Heller and
Suzanne Conklin Akbari**

A publication of the Dead Letter Office via
Ⓟ punctum books | earth, milky way

HOW WE READ: TALES, FURY, SOUND, NOTHING
Copyright ©2019 the editors and authors.
This work carries a Creative Commons BY-NC-SA 4.0 International license, which means that you are free to copy and redistribute the material in any medium or format, and you may also remix, transform and build upon the material, as long as you clearly attribute the work to the authors (but not in a way that suggests the authors or punctum books endorses you and your work), you do not use this work for commercial gain in any form whatsoever, and that for any remixing and transformation, you distribute your rebuild under the same license.
http://creativecommons.org/licenses/by-nc-sa/4.0/

First published in 2019 by dead letter office, BABEL Working Group, an imprint of punctum books, Earth, Milky Way.

ISBN-13: 978-1-950192-31-1 (print)
ISBN-13: 978-1-950192-32-8 (ePDF)
DOI: 10.21983/P3.0259.1.00
LCCN: 2019944175

Library of Congress Cataloging Data is available from the Library of Congress.

COVER ART: *The Tower Fable No. 1 — The Conclave of the Lighthouse: Black Brings His Queen*, Toronto and Boston ephemera, foil and paper, 10x12 in., Paula Billups, 2015. paulabillups.com

BOOK DESIGN: Chris Piuma. chrispiuma.com

All artwork within provided courtesy of the artists and photographers.

HIC SVNT MONSTRA

Table of Contents

xiii *Suzanne Conklin Akbari*
Introduction: Practicing Reading, Reading Practice

xxiii Who We Are

1 *Irina Dumitrescu*
Reading Lessons

13 *Anna Wilson*
I Like Knowing What is Going to Happen

25 *Suzanne Conklin Akbari*
Read It Out Loud

35 *Jessica Hammer*
From When We Read

47 *Lochin Brouillard*
De Vita Lochinis,
or Commentary on a Life of Reading

IMAGE: Emptying the carrels at Robarts Library, Toronto, ON.
PHOTO: Kaitlin Heller.

61 *Chris Piuma*
How I Read

73 *Stephanie Bahr*
How I Read, a History;
or "San Francisco Banking Contains No Trans Fats"

85 *Alexandra Atiya*
Text to Speech

97 *Jonathan Hsy*
Phantom Sounds

107 *Kirsty Schut*
On Not Being a Voracious Reader

117 *Kaitlin Heller*
Sleeping under the Mountain

131 *Jennifer Jordan*
Reading to Forget, Reading to Remember

141 *Brantley Bryant*
Best Practice Tips and Strategies for Academic
Reading to Maximize Your Time and Productivity

153 *Kaitlin Heller*
Afterword: The Parlor Scene

Suzanne Conklin Akbari

Introduction
Practicing Reading, Reading Practice

In some ways, this book stands on its own; in other ways, it's a sequel — or, better, a companion — to *How We Write: Thirteen Ways of Looking at a Blank Page* (punctum, 2015). The two collections have parallel foci (how we write, how we read) that are at once deceptively simple and provocatively complex. As we learn to read, we sound out words; as we learn to write, we learn to shape letter forms and characters. But for many of us, the struggle to write — and, as we explore here, the struggle to read — never goes away, no matter how practiced we become. This is true, as many of the essays gathered below will relate, even for those who grew up as eager readers and who would instinctively say of themselves that they "love to read." Both collections bring together thirteen essays into a multifaceted whole; neither purports to tell others how *to* write or how *to* read, but rather how *we* write, how *we* read: how we actively do it, in the real world, with success or failure, whether the experience feels dysfunctional or blissful.

In other ways, however, *How We Read* is very different from *How We Write*, not least in terms of their process. *How We Write* came together in the period between late May and early September 2015 — a record time (as our publisher told us) from initial impulse to print volume. The process was organic, moving from a roundtable discussion to blog posts, online commentary, and social media, one essay generating another. This accretive quality was inspired by a comment made by one of the contributors, Michael Collins: "Posting something on a blog is kind of like pushing a pebble down a mountain. Often it just clatters down all alone. But sometimes other pebbles join and it becomes a wonderful landslide." This ethos fundamentally shapes the volume: "I asked Michael if we could use his 'pebble' — that is, his blog post — as the first essay.... The Table of Contents, accordingly, demarcates the ripples in the pond that arose from the pebble of Michael's blog post" (*How We Write*, xvii). *How We Read*, conversely, proceeded step by step, in a more deliberate way. Kaitlin and I experienced frustrations, had to make changes, incurred delays; but we also perceived moments of clarity, surpassing beauty, and enigma.

Why was this the case? It's because reading can be hard, in a way that is very different from the way that writing can be hard. We all understand why it might be hard to write, especially at a high level; why should it be hard to read? The experience of shame and frustration occasioned by the struggle to read is something very different from those we chronicled in *How We Write*. I tell my story here in the introduction, while others do so in the following essays. Kaitlin and I sought to include a wide range of stories about reading, from those at earlier stages of life and those further on, those whose reading experience is more normative and those whose reading experience comes through differently abled bodies. We wanted to hear about the vivid qualities of reading, the images that are called up and that some readers inscribe in their ornately produced commonplace books; and we wanted to hear about the aural qualities of reading, the reading experience as embodied sound. Instead of offering a summary of the essays in the introduction, we have chosen to instead reflect on them retrospectively in the afterword, modelling the reading process in our own editorial practice. Feel free to turn to the back, where Kaitlin will tell you how it all turns out! Or stay here with me, if you prefer to read from front to back.[1]

When I was a child, there was a very special pleasure in reading fast. My fourth-grade classroom had a strange kind of projector device (a tachistoscope) that was meant to improve our reading speed: it projected a single line of text on the wall, moving more or less rapidly (you could set the pace) until the passage was finished. Then you would complete questions designed to measure reading comprehension. I gamed that machine until I could read (or at least skim) about 1200 words a minute. It was a kind of trick, but it also produced a certain flavor of reading pleasure: a highly superficial, super-fast, super-shallow engagement with language.

In some ways, this facility turned out to be valuable. As the years ticked by, the ability to read a lot of text very quickly, retaining only what was essential, was a crucial strength. I encouraged others — first, peers; later, students — to develop this same skill, believing that it would help them as much as it had me, making it possible to manage very large amounts of text in a short period of time. But as you will have guessed, and as is always the case, there was a necessary trade off: could it be possible to

---

[1] Or start with our original blog post: Kaitlin Heller and Suzanne Akbari, "How We Read,"*In the Middle* (blog), October 3, 2017, http://inthemedievalmiddle.com/2017/10/how-we-read.html.

have that facility for quick reading, and also muster up the ability to slow it down, to read in a deliberate, careful way? Up to a certain point, it was absolutely possible to maintain those two modes. But like Kaitlin, who describes in moving terms, in her essay below, what it was like to lose (terrifyingly) the ability to read for pleasure, I also came to a point where I could no longer hold these two modes in tension. It became extremely difficult to read deliberately, slowly, closely.

And the painful poignancy of this lay in the fact that those moments of deliberate, slow reading were among the most precious moments of my intellectual and, I would say, spiritual formation. To read highly compressed, distilled language — whether poetic verse (Whitman; Stevens) or sacred scripture (Leviticus; the Qur'an) — is to exit linear time, if only for a moment, to be in a separate in-between place where chronology stops mattering and you fully inhabit the single moment. Losing — or, at least, almost completely losing — that ability was terribly painful, and I am still working, right now, to try to get it back. One thing that has helped me to do so is remembering what it was to read slowly. These remembered experiences include the time of learning, both in college and in grad school, how to practice close reading (both times with a focus on seventeenth-century English poetry and prose), as well as older, more primal experiences of reading. In particular, I have been remembering what it was like to read as a very young child, including both my own memory of learning to read, and my memories of teaching children in my family to read. I tell some of these stories below, in my essay "Reading Out Loud." Healing memories in themselves, they might also be stories that are good for sharing, and good for thinking with as we reckon with our own histories of reading, and our reading practices.

The other thing that has helped me to once again take pleasure in reading is *The Spouter-Inn*, a literature podcast that I've been doing with Chris Piuma since January 2019.[2] On *The Spouter-Inn*, I am able to tell the story, and also tell about the story, and also tell my story: that is, both how the story seems to me and, sometimes, in the in-between spaces, to tell a little bit of my own story. We started with Homer's *Iliad*, and our most recent recording was Gertrude Stein's *Autobiography of Alice B. Toklas*. My goal, in this project, was to help others to read; I didn't realize that it would help me to rediscover my own joy in reading.

In a way, this reading podcast grows out of a course I developed at the University of Toronto in 2009, "The Literary Tradition." This was a big, year-long lecture course that the English Department decided to offer as a kind of 'backgrounds to English literature' requirement that undergraduates could take at the entry level. In the first year, we had about 400 students and nine teaching assistants to carry out tutorials that would supplement the lectures, which I gave in a large theatre space on campus. It was a strange experience teaching that course. Because the room was so big, I couldn't teach in the way I was accustomed to, with short periods of lecturing punctuated by interactive discussion. Instead, I had to take on what I can only describe as a 'preacherly mode,' where my aim was not just to convey information about the books we were reading, but to inspire. What I wanted to inspire was, exactly, love of

---

2 *The Spouter-Inn* is at https://www.megaphonic.fm/spouter, along with the other "fancy little shows" at Megaphonic (https://www.megaphonic.fm/).

reading: a desire to read more, to read widely, to read more than was required—a desire to keep reading even after the course was over. Over the next few years, I taught the class in slightly different ways, changing up the books. Homer's *Iliad*, Plato's *Symposium*, and the *Thousand and One Nights* were constants, but other books came and went—Augustine's *Confessions*, Goethe's *Faust*. But one thing stayed the same, and that was the remarkable power of the lecture, at certain moments, to create a sense of excitement in the room. This did not happen every time, of course; but when it did, the room was electric.

I started to want to find a way to do for casual readers something like what I had found I could do for the students in the Literary Tradition class, to build up a sense of excitement and a desire to read. Because I had already been writing headnotes to some of the same literary works, as part of my work as a volume editor for the *Norton Anthology of World Literature*, I thought that the obvious solution was a volume of essays. I thought I would call it "Dante's Friends," riffing off a striking moment that happens early in Dante's *Inferno*, where Dante (the character) enters Limbo and meets a whole range of poets, philosophers, and rulers from the ancient world. Dante is delighted when those ancient writers—Homer, Plato, and Ovid among them—welcome him among their number, calling him "poet." These essays, I thought, would be a way to bring out the conversations that happen across books over time, a conversation that Dante imaginatively brings to life in the account of Limbo in his *Inferno*.

I didn't want the essays to be lectures in written format. I wanted them to excite and engage the reader, and figured out that the way to do this was to foreground my own emotional response to these books, doing in writing what

I had been able to do spontaneously in the lecture. What I needed to do was to explain how these books resonated for me, why they mattered, how they made me feel. Accordingly, I began to consider how to integrate the personal within the professional, mingling scholarly insights with personal anecdotes. After roughing out a couple of these essays, I began to talk with friends about what I was trying to do. They consistently responded in the same way: politely interested in what I said about the books, their attention caught more by the personal stories I was using to put the books in context. This, I knew right away, could not work: I wanted my own response to support the books, not to upstage them.

I put the project aside, hoping that a solution would come to me if I left it alone for a while. Then one day, Chris—whom I'd told all about the collection of essays I was trying to write, and who had been involved in the Literary Tradition course long before—suggested, Maybe you could do what you're aiming to do through a podcast? I was intrigued, but uncertain; this was not a medium I had any sense of, either as a producer or a user of podcasts. But we kept talking, and before long, we had hatched a new project: *The Spouter-Inn*. Here, there was a way to harness the personal and the affective in the service of the books, a way to be very personal and yet also keep the words of the writers front and center.

When we plan out a podcast, Chris and I don't write a script: some podcasts, especially those that serve as teaching aids, do carefully compose and edit a script, and the producers will record and re-record until they get each episode exactly right. That's almost the opposite of what we do at *The Spouter-Inn*. We're aiming for spontaneity and a sense of excitement, so what we do is make a 'road map' listing a few basic turns that we'd like to take, and I add a handful of quotations that I think we might use. We never use all of the quotations, and we never do them in the order that I've listed. What we do is talk, and laugh, and think, and wonder. That's exactly the kind of feeling I was hoping to capture in those essays, and it's tantalizing to feel that Chris and I are beginning to make that hope a reality. We've completed our first cluster of three books so far — Homer's *Iliad*, Plato's *Symposium*, and Ovid's *Metamorphoses* — and we're in the midst of our second cluster, made up of books by three women writers: Christine de Pizan's *City of Ladies*, Louisa May Alcott's *Little Women*, and Gertrude Stein's *Autobiography of Alice B. Toklas*. I have a lot to say about what it might mean to make up a cluster of women writers — above all, why would we want to treat 'women writers' as a separate category at all? — and Chris and I will keep talking about the idea of a 'canon,' of 'great books,' or 'foundational' works. What do those terms imply, and how can we talk about the system of values, both implicit and explicit, that they convey? In the coming months, we have clusters planned on Evil, on America, on Revolution, on Frametales, and on Art Objects. We are thinking about a 'watery cluster,' with three books that say something about the Ocean. I haven't been this excited about reading, and about discussing what I've read, in a long time: it's like being a kid at the library again. I don't mean to be naïve; it's not always perfect. But it is sometimes joyful, in a way that at once feels familiar and utterly new.

In some ways, which I'll unpack a bit more in my own essay on "Reading Out Loud," *The Spouter-Inn* and *How We Read* are twins: they both emerge out of a phase when I was struggling to read, whether for work or for pleasure, and they both emerge out of a collaboration. The collaboration with Chris has been aural, while the collaboration with Kaitlin has been mediated through written text, but both of them have been both generative and renewing. In our conversations over the course of making this book, Kaitlin and I have already learned quite a bit about how our own histories of reading — both our deep histories and our proximate, urgent histories — inform our teaching and research practices, as well as how they have shaped us on a deeply personal level. Do teaching and research inhabit a different environment within our sensibility, totally divided from our pleasure reading, or are these domains contiguous or even overlapping? Is reading a fundamentally passive act — made visible in that strip of words flowing through the projector's light — or is it active? Is reading an act of consumption or an act of creation? Our hope, in bringing together these essays, is that they will allow you, Reader, to discover (or re-discover) the pleasure that lies in this most solitary of acts — which is also, paradoxically, the act of most complete plenitude.

Who We Are

IRINA DUMITRESCU writes and studies literature. She is the author of *The Experience of Education in Anglo-Saxon Literature* (Cambridge University Press, 2018), and the editor of *Rumba Under Fire: The Arts of Survival from West Point to Delhi* (punctum, 2016) and, with Eric Weiskott, *The Shapes of Early English Poetry: Style, Form, History* (Medieval Institute Publications, 2019). She is currently thinking about charisma, imperfection, and language learning. You can find her essays at irinadumitrescu.com.

ANNA WILSON is an Assistant Professor at Harvard University in one part of her reading life. She does not share her other name in non-fandom spaces because she doesn't want her students to be able to find her deeply earnest love stories about robots.

SUZANNE CONKLIN AKBARI is Director of the Centre for Medieval Studies at the University of Toronto, but would rather be working on her new project on medieval ideas of periodization, "The Shape of Time," and/or lying on the beach in North Truro. Her books include *Seeing Through the Veil: Optical Theory and Medieval Allegory*

IMAGE: Wall of glass bottles, City Museum, St. Louis.
PHOTO: Kaitlin Heller.

(University of Toronto Press, 2004), *Idols in the East: European Representations of Islam and the Orient, 1100–1450* (Cornell University Press, 2009), and four collections of essays, including *How We Write: Thirteen Ways of Looking at a Blank Page* (punctum, 2015). She is also a co-editor of the *Norton Anthology of World Literature* (4th ed.), and a master of structured procrastination.

JESSICA HAMMER is the Thomas and Lydia Moran Assistant Professor of Learning Science at Carnegie Mellon University, where she studies how playful experiences can change players' lives. Her work has been supported by the NSF, Amazon, the Heinz Foundation, Google, and other organizations. In 2018 she won Carnegie Mellon's Teaching Innovation Award for her work on peer feedback. She is also an award-winning game designer.

LOCHIN BROUILLARD is a doctoral candidate at the Centre for Medieval Studies at the University of Toronto. She started off her undergraduate degree telling her friends she wouldn't take any courses in medieval history. Now her dissertation focuses on familial conversions and spiritual kinship in medieval saints' Lives. She has been published in venues such as the *Journal of Medieval Monastic Studies*. Her research is in many ways guided by what she enjoys reading.

CHRIS PIUMA is a poet, musician, book designer, former academic, and more. He now spends most of his time on the Megaphonic podcast network. With Suzanne Conklin Akbari, he hosts *The Spouter-Inn; or, A Conversation with Great Books*, available at megaphonic.fm/spouter or through any reputable podcast app.

STEPHANIE BAHR is Assistant Professor of Literature at Hamilton College. Her work on *Titus Andronicus* and Reformation interpretive violence has appeared in *Shakespeare Quarterly*, and her work on rape and reading in *The Faerie Queene* is forthcoming in *Studies in Philology*. Her book project examines the interrelations of Reformation hermeneutics, sectarian violence, and Renaissance literature. Inspired partly by her own idiosyncratic reading experience, Bahr is fascinated by how people past and present interact with texts. In the classroom, she seeks to inspire a similar fascination by introducing students to codicology, paleography, and even basic book-binding.

ALEXANDRA ATIYA is a PhD student at the Centre for Medieval Studies at the University of Toronto. Her research focuses on late medieval English drama and she is interested in the relationship between text and performance. She received her MA from CMS in 2015 and her BA in History from Harvard in 2007. Prior to starting the PhD, Alexandra wrote fiction and poetry and contributed finance and arts journalism to various publications. She is currently working on a novel and co-authoring a graphic novel with Salman Toor, the artist whose painting forms the frontispiece of her essay.

JONATHAN HSY teaches at George Washington University, and he enjoys reading, writing, and scheming with collaborators. He is co-director (with Candace Barrington) of *Global Chaucers* and co-editor of its special issue of *Literature Compass* (2018), co-editor (with Mary-Kate Hurley and A.B. Kraebel) of the "Thinking Across Tongues" special issue of *postmedieval* (2017), co-editor (with Tory V. Pearman and Joshua R. Eyler) of Bloomsbury's forthcoming

A Cultural History of Disability in the Middle Ages, and co-facilitator (with Julie Orlemanski) of an ongoing crowd-sourced bibliography on race and medieval studies. He is also competing a short book on race and global medievalism, and a longer book on disabled medieval authors and their modern-day disabled audiences.

KIRSTY SCHUT defended her doctoral dissertation at the University of Toronto's Centre for Medieval Studies in March 2019. She holds an MA from the same institution and a Bachelor of Humanities from Carleton University, and — relevant to her essay in this collection — she studied Literary Arts at Canterbury High School in Ottawa. She has taught medieval history at the University of Toronto and Carleton University. Her research deals with late medieval intellectual history, concentrating on the fourteenth-century Dominican theologian John of Naples, and her publications include articles in *Recherches de Théologie et Philosophie Médiévales* and *Archivum Fratrum Praedicatorum*. For the last six years, she has shared an apartment in Toronto's Greektown with the excellent Emma Meadley Dunphy and gone contra dancing at every opportunity.

KAITLIN HELLER has held a lot of jobs that require reading, including a postdoc at Syracuse University, an editorial position at Del Rey Books, and a brief stint as a shelf reader in Widener Library. Heller stopped watching *Game of Thrones* several years ago but did finally finish *A Dance with Dragons*. Anne, if you're reading this: I thought it was good.

JENNIFER JORDAN is currently a doctoral student of Medieval History at SUNY Stony Brook. She will defend her dissertation, "'In her own dialect': Women, Gender, and Borders in Norman Sicily and Southern Italy," which examines women's movement, exchange, and identity, next year. She has published on pedagogy in *TEAMS* and has contributed performances to the *Performing Medieval Narrative Today* database (mednar.org). Outside of her academic work, she is the co-author with Sophie Goldstein of the award-winning webcomic *Darwin Carmichael Is Going to Hell*, and of the forthcoming *An Embarrassment of Witches* from Top Shelf Comics.

BRANTLEY BRYANT is Professor of English at Sonoma State University. He has published on Middle English literature and politics, Middle English literature and ecocriticism, and on adaptations of the medieval in popular culture.

How We Read

Irina Dumitrescu

Reading Lessons

I have forgotten how to read. It isn't the first time. I have forgotten before and I will forget again. In other words, I am still learning how to read.

"Read," like "love" or "think," has a thousand meanings pressed into one deceptively elementary verb. We use it in a way that tends towards simplicity. It is the connection of sounds and concepts to standardized squiggles, to trails of ink on squares of paper, scratches carved into sticks, glowing lines of curved neon, careful stitches poked through a tight canvas. It can seem a basic skill, at least to those who have left the learning of letters behind.

Watching my son learn to read now, I begin to understand how daunting a task it is, even given a phonetic language with a small alphabet, even with all the plasticity of a child's brain at his disposal. Learning to read is a years-long series of internalizing rules and then their many exceptions, of tiny modulations and adjustments. At first I thought it would be a matter of recognising twenty-six letters. Then I saw that he must navigate upper and lower cases, print and cursive, different typefaces and hands, the sounds rendered by certain combinations of letters, umlauts and double S's, unmarked short and long vowels,

IMAGE: Siesta Key, Florida. PHOTO: Anne Latowsky.

and the vagaries of foreign words and their unpredictable pronunciations.

So much work requires attention. My son approaches the challenge of decoding the world with intense concentration, straining to squeeze out meaning from each word and image. He is spellbound with anything legible, whether a phrase in bold, clear type or a comic strip that communicates just enough plot to fascinate, and will stare at it for what feels like ages. He is laboring hard, I know, but I still envy his power of absorption. Sometimes it feels like my practice as a reader has made me faster, but not consistently better. When I think of my own journey of learning to read, I am in fact thinking of a long process of learning and forgetting how to be with texts slowly, intimately, deeply.

My Eden was adolescence. As a teenager, I felt out of place, born in the wrong time, in the wrong body, and most inconveniently, in the wrong family and class. And like so many other young people, I searched with hungry desperation for some justification of my longings and inclinations in books. There were certainly distractions in that pre-internet paradise, but I also experienced flashes of grace, spaces of half an hour here and there when I could connect so directly to the language of a poem that it felt as though an electric charge were surging back and forth between my heart and the page. I was not so much reading the text as being read by it, imprinted by it, explained and forgivingly understood by those elegant patterns of ink. No doubt hormones played a part, but back then, those moments of communion with poetry (for it was usually poetry) felt sacred, all the more precious because unbiddable.

When I went to university the experience of reading shifted from romance to gymnastics. Yet formal exercise brings its own thrills. In the treatise on virginity he wrote for the nuns of Barking, the seventh-century English poet Aldhelm describes a series of gymnastic exercises Olympian athletes might undertake. In panting prose he imagines sweaty, oil-smeared wrestlers writhing, javelin-throwers guiding their projectiles, runners glorying in their victorious laps, riders urging forward their bloodied steeds, and rowers pressing through the sea. Then comes the twist: these are all metaphors for internal activities of the mind, and especially for the discipline of reading Scripture.

From the perspective of an early medieval intellectual, there wasn't much point in learning to read if you were going to stop at the surface of the text, content with its literal meaning. True literacy was a probing, analytical skill. It required reflecting on the etymologies of words, being attentive to puns and other kinds of soundplay, noticing patterns and parallels, comparing different versions of the same narrative, even unscrambling letters and counting sections of a text. What Aldhelm noticed — and I suspect he would have thought of all reading this way, not just of the Bible — was that reading was a bundle of related abilities, each of which needed precise training.

Studying for my English degree at the University of Toronto felt like being one of Aldhelm's athletes, rehearsing the various games at their stations. We tend to think of undergoing a course of study in terms of gathering material: learn the canon, from *Beowulf* to Virginia Woolf, memorize the periods and the movements and the big ideas. But so many of the literary works I encountered at Toronto demanded individual treatment, asked me to experiment with placements of body and habits of mind in order to approach them.

Take Milton (some might add: please). In my first-year introduction to the genres of English literature, Milton made me stumble. Our instructor had assigned several books of *Paradise Lost* in the fall semester, and I simply could not get into his verse. I had been an avid reader throughout high school, but had never encountered syntax as convoluted and formal as his. I could not concentrate enough to read beyond a few lines at a time. My freshman year was full of boisterous, boozy entertainments, and despite his stentorian voice, Milton could hardly be heard over the noise.

When I went home for Christmas, however, I decided to give Milton another go, and took my little Everyman edition with me to the bath. There was something about being immersed in nearly scalding water that took away just enough of my resistance to him. Suddenly, almost like magic, I could flow into the pentameters of *Paradise Lost*, follow sentences without hesitation as they spilled from one line into another, be swept away by the sheer cascading sound of it. After that, Milton was unlocked. I did not need to be in a bath to read him, I simply had to surrender in the same way, to submerse myself in the rhythm of his language. He became one of my favorite authors, as much for the overwhelming feeling of reading him as for the intellectual world he built in his epic.

University, I realized, was as much about learning to read as it was about actually reading things. I felt a thrill every time an instructor taught me the tricks of a text; these seemed like the real secrets I had come for. When I told my utterly dignified professor of Romantic literature that I was having trouble getting through Coleridge's *Biographia Literaria*, she smiled enigmatically and said she had always found a dram of scotch helpful for absorbing that particular work.

My political philosophy prof was of the Straussian school, and taught us to assume intention in great works even when we found what seemed like errors. It was a humbling but powerful lesson for me at the time, since I had read Plato in my early teens and thought his arguments illogical and deeply silly. How exciting to see I had been wrong, to find sense where I had mainly seen nonsense, to trace the rhetoric of deliberate mistakes throughout a work. When I went back to Leo Strauss much later I found out there was a framework for the reading practice with which I did not agree, and I do think even the great minds of the ages can make mistakes. But the exercise of assuming sense as a starting position proved to be a valuable one when I encountered early medieval literature, so often anonymous, so often assumed by scholars to be corrupted or obscure or naive.

Still, most of the lessons took place in my spare time, as a result of my own passions and frustrations and experiments. I remember having a particularly hard time with Wordsworth's *Prelude* one semester. We had been reading other Romantic poets in the course; next to Byron and Shelley and Keats, Wordsworth was dry as dust. Now, Milton had been difficult, but *Paradise Lost*, with its celestial battlefields and charismatic Satan, was at least dramatic. When it came to Wordsworth, I simply could not understand why he had bothered to write in the first place if he couldn't think of anything exciting to put in the poetry. And given how boring *The Prelude* was, why would he subject me to three versions of it?

Determined to do my duty, I took my Penguin Classic along on my winter vacation to Florida, hoping to force myself through somehow. On one particular day, the relatives I was visiting drove me to a beach so I could at least have a look at the ocean even if it was too cold to swim. I began to pace slowly on the flat sand, and as I did, it occurred to me to pull *The Prelude* out of my purse and open the book. The slow tempo of my walking started to align itself with the languid pace of Wordsworth's meter. Once my feet and his were synchronized, I was able to follow his meaning too.

This eureka moment did not help me love Wordsworth, but it gave me the key to reading him — from then on, I would pace as I read him. A little while later I read William Hazlitt's essay "On My First Acquaintance with Poets," and was stunned to find his description of Wordsworth's method of composition. "Coleridge has told me," writes Hazlitt, "that he himself liked to compose in walking over uneven ground, or breaking through the straggling branches of a copse-wood; whereas Wordsworth always wrote (if he could) walking up and down a straight gravel walk, or in some spot where the continuity of his verse met with no collateral interruption." To read Wordsworth's verse, I had had to imitate the movements of his body as he composed it.

The hardest reading challenge for me was drama. It wasn't difficult to get through per se, or even to understand the plot or figurative language. I spent the first summer of university working as a secretary and speed-read the collected plays of Shakespeare in a window on my computer when there were no other tasks to do. But I almost never picture what I read, so even when reading plays carefully I forget which line belongs to which character, what they might be doing as they speak it, or who else might still be standing silently on the stage.

My crash course in reading dramatic texts made me, ironically, a terrible student for an entire semester. A good friend and I were tasked with directing our college's fall play. We chose *Love's Labour's Lost*, and dove into preparing an elaborate outdoor production at the expense of our schoolwork. I rapidly grasped the difference between reading a play and putting one on stage. When actors did not understand what a particular line meant, they asked us, and the entire rehearsal stopped while they stared at us expectantly and we racked our brains. When writing an essay on a literary work, I could choose to discuss the passages I understood best and ignore the ones that were still opaque. But performing Shakespeare meant acting the hard parts too: every line needed an interpretation, because every line needed to be delivered with meaning. At the same time, watching our student actors rehearse I began to understand how Shakespeare's lines worked as stage directions too. The more gifted actors instinctively carried out the gestures and movements written into the play's text, just as Early Modern actors were trained to do.

My reading lessons could be purely cognitive, curiously embodied, or startlingly emotional. During my bachelor's degree, I began learning Old English, then Latin. These were perhaps the most literal reading lessons I received in undergrad, and they turned out to have a surprising affective component. When I took Toronto's year-long course in Old English, I had not started a new language in any kind of serious way for over a decade. Old English meant learning a lot of abstract grammar from a frankly difficult textbook — in short, it was hard going at times. Still, I fell in love with it for its difficulty, and I remember the precise moment when that happened.

I was studying for our final exam in the course, and had taken my books to our college library to retranslate all the poetry we had read and make sure I had it right. Being, to put it mildly, extremely pretentious, I was writing out the translations with my fountain pen, which I pompously insisted on dipping into my inkpot instead of using cartridges like a peasant. One mournful poem, *The Wanderer*, was slow going. As I struggled to work out the syntax, each individual word had time to occupy my attention, had space to bloom in my imagination. It wasn't simply that, for once, I could picture what the elegy described. I could feel what the exile felt, the icy cold of the sea biting his fingers, the warm sense of homecoming as he placed his forehead on his lord's knee in his dream, the devastation of waking up and seeing it all gone. I looked down at my notepad and saw that my tears had bled the ink, rendering my translation illegible.

Learning a new language, a moderately difficult one, had given me the power of concentration I could not muster on my own. It had made me a child in a sense. More than that, by forcing me to struggle to access even the basic meaning of the line, it gave me that pure, profound connection to poetry that I have spent much of my life longing for. Once I became better at reading Old English it lost some of its emotional kick — it took less from me and gave me less in return.

My Anglo-Saxon friend Aldhelm had a penchant for composing extremely difficult Latin, full of obscure Greek borrowings and over-the-top alliteration. This so-called hermeneutic Latin became a fashion in some learned circles in the early Middle Ages, and it is sometimes thought to be an in-group marker: it wasn't enough to learn Latin as a second tongue, you were *really* part of the club if you could manage to read and write a perversely hard form of the language. Given my own experience, I wonder if there wasn't something else at stake too, if Anglo-Saxons did not also feel that they had lost something as their Latin skills improved. Perhaps hermeneutic Latin was a way to recapture the precious attention demanded by texts that are hard, to regain the emotional immediacy that accompanies painfully slow reading.

Most of my reading lessons ended with my undergraduate education. Since then, the circumstances of my life have increasingly pushed me to read faster, at the cost of comprehension and depth. In the process of becoming a researcher and a teacher of literature, I learned to plow through piles of scholarly articles each week, to scan a German or Italian book for the sections that might be useful to my thesis, to skim a literary text I had already taught a few times just to jog my memory. But while I was being trained to dissect imaginative literature with scientific precision, I lost the knack for reading it.

For years, I have found it difficult to get into a novel. Entering a new imaginative world feels like too much effort, so when I read for pleasure, I choose nonfiction. As a teenager I encountered the old stereotype that made-up stories are for the young and frivolous (and often female), while nonfiction is for the old and serious (and probably male). Now that I pay taxes and pluck out my grey hairs, I am convinced that fiction is the more demanding genre. Poetry, the great romance of my pubescent years, feels even more distant, requiring focus and receptivity I can rarely muster. Sometimes I wonder if the young read novels and poems because they are the only ones who can.

My body used to help me find my way into difficult texts; it was a matter of synchronizing it, aligning it, relaxing it to accept the words. Curiously, it is still my body that allows me to find my way back to literature now and then, though now it does so by breaking down. Here I am in a daze of postpartum trauma, hunching over my nursing newborn for hours. I cannot recognise my own home or tell the time of day, but somehow I can be entranced by Elizabeth Barrett Browning's *Aurora Leigh*, a verse epic to women's creative power and the best mommy advice book I could have. Or here, I am confined to bed by bronchitis. Released from all the stultifying duties of adult life, I plunge into a pile of novels, feeling guiltily fortunate to be allowed hours on end to read. Or now, in the midst of a weekend dance workshop in a strange city, I find myself lying on the creaky bed of my small hotel room, my muscles screaming and slathered in ointment, aching too much to sleep or even watch television. I open Samina Ali's *Madras on Rainy Days*, and its soft lyricism hypnotises me deep into the night. It is as though I now have to lose a bit of my own corporeal solidity to enter a novel or a poem.

A clue for why this might be lies in an outlandish Old English poem I have spent years trying to understand, *Solomon and Saturn*. It is a dialogue between two legendary men: Solomon, the wise king of Israel, and Saturn, a wealthy student who has traveled through India, Greece, and Libya. Saturn offers his twelve sons and a wealth of gold if he can learn the Lord's Prayer — a strange text to make such a big deal of, given what common knowledge it would have been for Christians at the time the poem was written. The Lord's Prayer, or *Pater Noster*, was among the very first things someone might learn to read if they had the opportunity at all, right after getting to know the alphabet. To be accurate, Saturn does not ask to be taught the prayer itself. Instead, he asks to be "gebrydded" by the prayer, and scholars are not quite certain what "gebrydded" means. They think it might mean "frightened," or perhaps "terrified," or less weirdly, "shaken" or "overawed."

Solomon seems happy enough to help Saturn out. He tells Saturn all about the magical powers of the Lord's Prayer, how it heals the sick and teaches scripture and opens the doors of heaven. And then he does something even more bizarre: he describes how, when a person sings the prayer, each one of its letters transforms into a little warrior. In this bookish Anglo-Saxon scene of mortal combat, the fighting letters torture demons in brutally memorable ways: T stabs a devil in the throat and shatters his jaws, R shakes a demon by the hair until its limbs are out of joint, while S slams one of his enemies against a stone so hard that his teeth fly out.

It struck me at some point that this is a poem about learning to read. Yes, it is about understanding the individual letters on a page, but it is also about developing a powerful connection to a lyric, a story, a prayer or a song. *Solomon and Saturn* imagines that a text can grab the reader so profoundly and emotionally that the act of encountering it might feel like terror. I do not think that the bookish Anglo-Saxon who wrote this curious poem really wanted reading to feel scary or violent. But I think he — or she — found a poetic way to express how shattering deep reading can be, and how our very bodies sometimes have to be a little bit destroyed for us to access it. The poet also knew there was something implausible and magical about reading intensely, that the feeling might only be granted for brief moments, like a spell.

Yes, I have forgotten how to read. I have practice at forgetting, but practice in learning too. And occasionally I am reminded that I belong to a quiet, timeless community of other longing readers, all of them yearning for a connection perfect and ephemeral. With them, I am still learning how to read.

Anna Wilson

I Like Knowing What Is Going to Happen

When I first started regularly staying over at my then-girlfriend, now-wife's tiny Toronto apartment, I was struck by the romances; piles of them, everywhere, with titles like *The Duke's Baby*, *To Love a Sheikh*, *He Was Her Boss*, *The Greek Millionaire and the Reluctant Bride*. In our new home, a slightly larger apartment in Cambridge, MA, the sediment of clean-cut heroes and swept-back heroines is already beginning to build up. They are always in my peripheral vision, on the nightstand, on the tables and desks, underfoot, in her handbag for train journeys. She eats them up, unapologetically and at speed. Sometimes I tease her, "Are they going to get together?" and she squeaks, "I don't know!"

She does know, of course, and if she isn't sure, she flips to the back to check. Her orbit makes it easier to resist the gravitational pull of the canon which has regimented the environments in which I read professionally. I now work in an Ivy League English department, and find myself renegotiating insecurities I felt as an undergraduate at Cambridge and a new graduate student at the University of Toronto, desperate both to be and to appear as well read as my peers.

Being educated in non-American contexts on the one hand and being a medievalist who came by way of Classics on the other exacerbates this anxiety about appearing undereducated, uncultured, missing a few steps among my colleagues working on David Foster Wallace, Emily Dickinson, or even Spenser, in addition to the typically medievalist sense of the precarity and minoritization of our field within an increasingly presentist academy. But at the heart of my anxiety about my adequacy as a professional reader is that since I was sixteen, the vast majority of my reading for pleasure has been in the romance-heavy, culturally denigrated, overwhelmingly gendered genre of fanfiction.

I have been thinking a lot, in this other Cambridge, about my undergraduate experience. I fell in love with scholarship. I was at times desperately unhappy. And I read so much fanfiction. I would read thousands of words a day of it, and when I wasn't reading it, I was writing it. The same two men, unlikely companions in a mission to another galaxy (I was into *Stargate: Atlantis* at the time), misfits thrown together over and over in all sorts of tragicomical ways, falling in love again and again. The variety was in the situation, and even the situations themselves became clichés to be unwound and folded in on themselves, a Mandelbrot of romance: alien sex rituals, forced to pose as master and servant, near-death experience in malfunctioning spaceship, trapped in a cave and it's cold and oh no, there's only one sleeping bag ... snappy dialogue, sex scenes, and a happy ending promised and delivered, every time.[1]

---

1   I feel that citing specific stories here would somewhat defeat the point: I cite instead fanfiction en masse. You can find a lot of it at https://archiveofourown.org, http://www.fanfiction.net, or http://www.wattpad.com.

—§—

There are (broadly speaking) two schools of thought in the fanfiction communities in which I have participated, which are English-speaking, online, and largely focused on western media: to warn, and not to warn. There's an unvarying common ground philosophy across those two schools: "don't like, don't read." The to-warn school, broadly informed by second-wave feminism but with its own history (content or trigger warnings have been under debate in fandom for decades), advocates for a curatable experience.[2] Fanfiction is tagged and labelled, allowing archives to be searched for stories featuring specific pairings, tropes, sex acts, kinks, and subgenres that prioritize the kinds of feelings a reader might look for: grief (deathfic), catharsis (hurt/comfort), arousal (PWP, an acronym variously expanded as "porn without plot" or "plot, what plot"), delight (crackfic). My favourite genre name — like all fanfiction terminologies, an ephemeral one, which has fallen out of common usage — is the escapist domestic fantasy of "curtainfic": not, as you might think, a story in which a metaphorical curtain falls — an ending, a death — but a story in which the protagonists go shopping for actual curtains. Bedsheets or flatware would be an acceptable substitute. In the ideal version of the to-warn philosophy, any polarizing content is labelled, and particular reading experiences are findable or avoidable. One person's trauma is another person's fun Sunday afternoon, but anyone should be able to find their own particular fun Sunday afternoon.

---

2   Alexis Lothian, "Choose Not To Warn: Trigger Warnings and Content Notes from Fan Culture to Feminist Pedagogy," *Feminist Studies* 42, no. 3 (2016): 743–56.

The not-to-warn school shares the opinion of the majority of the academy and literary establishment on trigger warnings: the reader puts themselves into the artist's hands. The reader is willing to be unsettled, to be surprised, even shocked. The reader should be ready to leave their comfort zone. But, in contrast to in the classroom, the not-to-warn school is also predicated on 'don't like, don't read': the idea that the reader can step away whenever they want, since they are reading entirely of their own volition, for pleasure. The archive I most frequent now — the Archive of Our Own, one of the three biggest online fanfiction archives[3] — has a content warnings system built into its story upload function, which authors can opt out of, and an additional freeform tagging system.[4] With the caveat that there are many things fanfiction writers committed to using content warnings may not notice or acknowledge in their own writing that readers may wish to avoid — racism being a primary example[5] — being a fanfiction reader is a highly controllable experience, if you want it to be. I like a lot of things about fanfiction, but this predictability, and, more than that, the commitment to my control over my own reading experience, even if not always ideally executed, not

---

3 At least as far as English-language fanfiction goes, although it does host fanfiction in other languages.

4 For the history of this controversial tagging system, see the Wiki page, "The AO3 Tagging Policy Debate," Fanlore.org, https://fanlore.org/wiki/AO3_Tagging_Policy_Debate, accessed 9/28/2018. For fanfiction metadata practices more generally, see Shannon Fay Johnson, "Fan Fiction Metadata Creation and Utilization within Fan Fiction Archives: Three Primary Models," *Transformative Works and Cultures* 17 (2014), https://journal.transformativeworks.org/index.php/twc/article/view/578.

5 Rukmini Pande, *Squee from the Margins: Fandom and Race* (Iowa City: University of Iowa Press, 2018).

only makes it something I enjoy when I can't enjoy much else, but also has empowered me to ask of myself: what exactly *do* I like? This thing in this story that I liked, does it have a name? And can I get more? To become proficient at this kind of curated reading of fanfiction is to learn to theorize one's own reading experience.[6] To taxonomize.

— § —

Anxiety, for me, is a sonic experience; it's a howling wind just out of my hearing range, sometimes barely there, sometimes drowning out everything else (such times are rare at the moment, thankfully). Life unsettles me. At times when my baseline level of anxiety is medium to high, I can hardly stand to read most things, let alone sign up for experiences where I can't leave the room or stop at will — theatre is out of the question, unless I've read the play before, and I'll avoid movies or even live music. When all I want is to feel safe, I have learned to distrust art. It isn't just that artists think too little of slaughtering a woman to make a minor point, although that's part of it. The whole idea on which much modern literature is predicated — that the reader meets an unknown cast of characters and goes on a journey with them to an unknown end point — makes

---

6 Such theorization is known as "meta" in the fan community, and it appears in blog and social media posts, on the AO3 (tagged 'meta'), and in online publications. The now-defunct Livejournal community Metafandom (https://metafandom.livejournal.com/) functioned as a newsletter, collecting links to (mostly English-language) meta essays from among the larger fan community; no such centralized, comprehensive meta aggregator now exists to my knowledge, as fandom has grown and fragmented across social media platforms.

for an unpleasant experience for anxious me. Sometimes rewarding, yes. But rarely something I'd choose to do with my free time, to relax.

I read predictable, highly circumscribed genres almost exclusively — mystery is a favourite. Like romance, mystery offers a trajectory from chaos into order, from not-okay to okay. There are rules which are rarely broken: a crime was committed, the detective never dies, someone is guilty, the community is made cognizant of its sins and purged of them. The narrative of detection slowly resolves the narrative of the crime into its correct sequence, until the doubled temporal structure unwinds into a single linear thread from the events leading up to the crime to the identification and punishment of its culprits.[7] Arguably, romance too follows this pattern of the doubled timeline that must be resolved into a single linear narrative: the resolution and consummation relies on the unravelling of misunderstandings and misapprehensions, the unpacking of the protagonists' individual experiences into a shared view of their pasts in which all is known, all is understood, and the future is a single path walked together.

Slash fanfiction, too, in its traditional form, partakes of both the mystery and the romance. For decades, metaphors of detection have permeated the slash fan's reading activity: both playful and sophisticated, she picks out and recontextualizes textual clues to the "real" queer relationship between fictional characters, the depiction of which has been obscured by cultural censorship, and she resolves

---

7 Tzvetan Todorov, "The Typology of Detective Fiction," trans. Richard Howard, in *The Poetics of Prose* (Oxford: Blackwell, 1977), 42–52.

the evidence into a truth, achieving a victory of queerness over its own invisibility.[8]

Another highly specific fanfiction trope popular enough to appear in the playful taxonomies of fandom, and for which I retain a certain nostalgic fondness although it has now been largely rendered obsolete by changing attitudes to LGBTQ+ rights in fanfiction's cultural geography, is WNGWJLEO — "we're not gay, we just love each other." Classic 80s and 90s slash fanfiction imagined its macho male protagonists loving each other while exempt from the stressors and threats of homosexuality that dominated its sparse mainstream depictions; for some writers and readers, this was an escapist fantasy of romance without (or, with less) heterosexuality-assigned gender roles, with little or nothing to do with real gay experience or communities, sometimes in retrospect even actively homophobic; for others, it was an escapist fantasy of queer safety that appropriated the forms and style of the well-established genre of heterosexual romance and subverted mainstream depictions of homosociality that excluded queer love.[9] For me, a baby bi, it was both. Fanfiction makes to me a double promise of safety in content and form: that queer people will have happy endings, and that I already know what happens.

---

8   For an analysis of the way slash interacts with canon, see Ika Willis, "Keeping Promises to Queer Children: Making Space (for Mary Sue) at Hogwarts," in *Fan Fiction and Fan Communities in the Age of the Internet: New Essays*, ed. K. Hellekson and K. Busse (Jefferson, N.C.: McFarland and Co., 2006), 153–70.

9   For an unpacking of WNGWJLEO and its context, see Kristina Busse and Alexis Lothian, "A History of Slash Sexualities: Debating Queer Sex, Gay Politics, and Media Fan Cultures," in *The Routledge Companion to Media, Sex and Sexuality*, ed. Feona Attwood, Danielle Egan, Brian McNair and Clarissa Smith (London: Routledge, 2018), 117–29.

— § —

I think my restricted, curatorial, defensive, wary, comfort-seeking, affirmatory reading has made me a better reader, not a worse one. Looking back at the history of my own reading I can see how it is shaped around the silhouette of my anxiety: I've become acutely attuned to paratext, to the language of book reviews, to the shape of other people's taste, to the meaning of genre markers, style and form, to the nature of response. I am not what Ricoeur had in mind when he described certain kinds of critical reading as "hermeneutics of suspicion," but I am a suspicious reader. Is this book going to unsettle me so that I can't sleep? Is this going to be a pleasant way to spend my train ride, or will I give up after five minutes and be bored and rattled for the remaining two hours?

I can also see that my gravitation towards premodern literature — in my undergraduate Classics degree, in my later graduate career in medieval literature — has also been one towards a literature where the unknown does not dominate storytelling. Medieval literature surprises me all the time, I delight in its strangeness, but the ending is always already known. The dreamer will wake, the saint will be martyred, the knights will return to Arthur's court and reflect on what they have learned, the doomed lovers will die, Jesus will walk out the steps of his Passion. Chaucer's *Troilus and Criseyde* begins with a lament over its ending, and throughout, its chatty narrator exclaims his regret that he cannot change what is going to happen (since he has copied it all out of a book), even as we watch our hero Troilus meditate on the nature of fate and predestination, and our heroine Criseyde try to resist the reputation history has in store for her. Their resistance is futile:

everything that can happen to them has already happened. The creative energy goes into the combination of elements, the variations on a theme. Readerly uncertainty is almost completely absent as an artistic principle. And why shouldn't it be? What is so good about not knowing what is going to happen?

We tend to think of the movement from medieval to modernity in terms of progress, and this is no different in the field of literature: we learn to celebrate the move from adaptation to originality, from archetypes to individuals, from templates to open-form, as if this was the obvious and inevitable way forward. Not only does this ascribe inherent value to one particular, arbitrary literary choice, but it also casts by the wayside much, if not most, of modern literature as not what we mean when we say modern literature. I recall my wife pondering whether she could apply to a particular postdoctoral fellowship intended for research projects on identity in Canadian Literature. Her work was on the construction of Canadian identity by Canadian romance writers working for what was, at the time, the largest, most profitable, and arguably most culturally influential Canadian publisher: Harlequin.[10] But it was quite clear what they meant by Literature.

---

10 Jessica Taylor, "Flexible Nations: Canadian Romance Writers, American Romance, and the Romance of Canada" in *Reading between the Borderlines: Cultural Production and Consumption across the 49th Parallel*, ed. Gillian Roberts (Kingston: McGill-Queen's University Press, forthcoming). Nota bene: Harlequin was purchased by American media giant News Corp in 2014 and is now a subsidiary of HarperCollins, but it is still based in Toronto.

—§—

When people used to recommend literary fiction to me or force loans upon me, I used to lie and say I would definitely read it; I now say, with utmost gravity, "I'm afraid I don't read anything without dragons or spaceships." It's not strictly true. I do like fantasy and space adventures, the kind where the hero — preferably a tough-as-nails woman — will definitely live. I like books with telepathic unicorns. I like robots. I like magic. (When we talk about taking the reader out of their comfort zones, we never mean gravitational physics.) My taste in mystery is specific: no sexual violence; cats are okay; detective must not be of the "total fuckup who lives only for the job" variety; recipes at the end are ideal. I almost never like great literature, the kind that's described as "powerful." I don't want to have to hack my reading experience by flipping to the end; I want to know what's going to happen before I start, I want the author to know that I know, and I want the book to have been designed with that in mind.

The name I use in professional spaces has now sprouted an acronym before it and an institutional title after it. It doesn't fit right, and it's heavy; the name I use in fandom is very short. I am trying to bend the new space I find myself occupying into the right shape for me by being even more insistent — perhaps obnoxiously so — about the kind of reader I am. There's a tendency for moral valuations to creep in around reading the same way there is around eating, particularly for women (I'm reading trash, I'm ashamed of what I enjoy); I'm trying to weed that out of my vocabulary. I am slowly figuring out how to integrate content warnings into my teaching practice, because I have come to believe that while my role as an educator and a scholar is to disrupt preconceptions, including my own, there are also contexts in which offering safety — and holding myself accountable for that offer — is the most radical and difficult thing I can do. And I'm trying to build a relationship with my anxiety where I'm not angry with it for keeping me back from reading stuff that people say I should like and maybe I would like if I were a completely different person, but instead notice it as a shaping force in my taste, and question a literary hierarchy which values my fear more than my pleasure. Fuck that noise. I know what I like.

Suzanne Conklin Akbari

Read It Out Loud

The earliest memory I have is of reading out loud. My parents were high school graduates who believed that it was important to try to give their only child a good start in life, so they had bought a copy of the *Encyclopedia Britannica*, which came along with a multi-volume children's encyclopedia in red covers. Those books were the foundation of my early reading, because the back of each volume contained stories drawing on and referring to the alphabetic entries. My mother used to read those stories to me before bed and, one evening, sitting beside her on the couch, I got impatient for her to start reading (I think she was talking to my father) and started reading aloud myself. I remember the moment because both of my parents became alarmed — or that's what it seemed like to me. I was afraid I had done something wrong.

My father had a newspaper in his hand. Thinking that I must have memorized the story and was less reading than recalling, he said "Can you read this?" I read a few words, not all of them, but it was enough for my parents to get very excited. I gradually realized that I wasn't in trouble; on the contrary, my parents were delighted. I was four, and that moment shaped me as a reader. The joy in reading came partly from the book, getting lost in the story, but it also came from the reaction of those around me. There was a reward in reading, as my own actions were reflected — in positive or negative terms — in the reaction of others.

Reading out loud was fundamental to early childhood reading, but then it went underground. I read in my room; I read in a corner of the living room, in an old green recliner by the window, with a pile of books on the floor; I read at family gatherings, out of the way on a couch or a spare bedroom; I read in the mall, when my mother wanted to go shopping, and would park me on the floor near the clothes racks. That reading was silent and purely visual. Reading in school, too, was silent, whether in the form of the speed-reading projectors introduced in fourth grade or in the novel hidden inside my seventh-grade science textbook. As a Jehovah's Witness, with at least five hours of congregational meetings per week, I was also silently reading. Reading re-emerged from silence only when I went to university, where the classroom turned out to be a place where what had been purely visual experience suddenly became aural again.

The first place this happened was in a course on Joyce's *Ulysses* taught by Hugh Kenner. I wasn't enrolled in the course but some of my friends were, so I went along to many of the class meetings. Kenner had a way of conducting class that turned out to be my first introduction to how to teach, though I didn't know it at the time: while he would spend some of the period talking about the text or answering questions, much of the time was spent in simply reading *Ulysses* out loud. I cannot put into words how powerful that was. Kenner must have taken great care in choosing what passages to read, because our understanding of the work grew exponentially with every one of them. He read the words simply, almost in a monotone, rarely changing the pace or volume of his speech. Many years later, when I began to teach literature, I learned also to choose passages that would be powerful when read aloud, and to try to teach myself how to use my voice in order to ventriloquize the text — or, at least, my sense of the text — in a way that mirrored my experience in Hugh Kenner's classroom.

The second place this happened was in graduate school, in a course on English Renaissance poetry taught by Edward Tayler. I had taken a course with Tayler before, and so was familiar with his carefully constructed seminar format, which required students — usually two or three per week — to read out a textual analysis of one of the assigned works. In this particular course, however, we were focused on lyric poetry instead of the long narrative poetry or prose of the previous course; as a result, each presentation was focused on a single, self-contained lyric. One of the first presenters, Heidi Brayman, was about to begin reading, but paused briefly; she asked, "Do you mind if I read the poem out loud first?"

I remember the feeling in the room. At first, everyone almost held their breath; was this a juvenile, immature thing to ask? Would we be wasting valuable seminar time if she were to read out loud something that, after all, we had already read silently in preparing for class? We all looked at Tayler, who didn't say anything at all for a minute, but looked down at his notes, written on index cards. (His notes weren't just on that week's texts; they were about each of us, our interests and interpretive tendencies. If we ever do a book on *How We Teach*, I would write about Tayler's pedagogy, which I found utterly transformative, but which is also emphatically not the way I teach. There's a productive contradiction hidden there.) Then he raised his head, and his voice shook a little bit; he was visibly moved, and simply said, "Yes." After that, every one of us (without asking) read the poem out loud before we started our presentation. Like listening to Hugh Kenner read *Ulysses*, the experience of listening to fellow students reading the poems they had chosen was powerful. Reading it out loud did something unnameable, did a kind of interpretive work that was completely different from what we were doing when we analysed the structure or talked about the contexts in intellectual or social history. I didn't know what that work was, but it was clear to me that something was happening.

During the same year I was in Tayler's seminar, I was teaching my first child how to read. I had sometimes read to my little brother, but we were so far apart in age that I was out of the house when he was learning to read; because that experience was only occasional, I couldn't really observe his progress. It was completely different with my daughter, who loved her books so much that, at bedtime, she would fill an old basket with stuffed animals and a pile of little board books and paperbacks. Reading aloud to her every night was almost like song, because while some of the books were new acquisitions that would only gradually become familiar, others were favorites that we both had memorized. Those books were almost like songsheets. Even now, almost thirty years later, I can repeat the lines of Maurice Sendak's *Pierre*, or Sandra Boynton's *The Going to Bed Book*: "and down once more, but not so fast, they're on their way to bed at last."

I would read to her, and she would read to me, with the proportion of reading gradually shifting over time. Those were intensely intimate evenings, made so by the shared experience of reading. Reading to her younger siblings as these came along, and then reading to little cousins in later years, were echoes of that initial pleasure in reading out loud together, that narrative voice as song. Reading to a young cousin over a few weeks last summer echoed those experiences: we would take turns, sound out hard words, and — when the same book was read on consecutive nights — re-read with the same cadence and intonation, so that every night was a new performance of the song/text. This ritual, repetitive, almost liturgical kind of reading, especially evident with my own children, to whom I read most frequently and over long periods of time, had a powerful impact on two levels: it produced a sense of intimacy between we two readers, and it developed a kind of launch pad for solo reading, generating an almost audible internal voice for these new readers.

Though I never reproduced the reading aloud in graduate seminars that was a feature of Tayler's class, it was a fundamental feature of my undergraduate teaching as soon as I took up an academic job, drawing both on that shivery feeling in the graduate seminar and the long-ago memory of listening to Hugh Kenner read from *Ulysses*. In discussion classes, and even more in large lectures, the fundamental backbone of every class prep was the selection of passages. In smaller classes, I would sometimes read out a passage and sometimes ask a student to do so; in very large lectures, however, I would be the one to read out loud, taking care to choose passages that I knew would produce a powerful emotional response: Priam anticipating his ultimate fate, in the *Iliad*; Procne seeing the face of her son, Itys, in the *Metamorphoses*; Dante recognizing the face of his old teacher, Brunetto Latini, in the *Inferno*;

Caliban explaining the strange music on the "isle...full of noises" in the *Tempest*. I'm nearsighted and don't wear glasses, so in the 400-person lecture theatre, I could never see the faces of the students clearly. But I could always tell when their attention was on me, because of the feel of the room. When I was reading those passages, I could tell that they were rapt — at least sometimes, when I had chosen the passage well and my reading was strong. Here, reading was not just having an aural effect; it was having an affective effect, moving the students emotionally in a way that (I hoped) would stimulate their desire to read while also opening up their sense of curiosity in preparation for tutorial discussions and conversations outside of class.

The embodied effects of reading become evident when people read aloud. This is the case for the instructor standing before a large class; for the student reading a passage in the course of discussion; for the audience gathered in a bookstore to hear an author read their work; and for a cluster of readers gathered to read *Moby-Dick* at the New Bedford Whaling Museum in early January, or *Ulysses* in Dublin on Bloomsday. Online reading sites (e.g., http://www.mobydickbigread.com/), too, bring together readers and listeners, trading the image on the page for the impact on the ear. The power of reading aloud became most apparent to me not in the lecture hall, however, but in a smaller class; and it wasn't my own voice that created the effect, but rather my lack of a voice. I was teaching a British literature survey, and we had just begun to discuss metaphysical poetry; I had asked my students to read selections from Donne and Marvell in preparation for class. That morning, however, I woke up with laryngitis, unable to make any sound above a whisper. What to do? I came to class and wrote a brief explanation of my state on the board. Then I silently handed out a photocopy containing a few of that day's poems; once they were all distributed, I came over to one of the students and whispered, pointing to a stanza, "Read!"

She read. And then I whispered to her, "Say something about it." The students were bemused, a little puzzled at first as to how to respond, but they rose to the occasion. I went from student to student ("Read!") and asking, in a whisper, for more. This was a strange occasion, not repeatable, but it taught me a lesson about the power of reading. I learned to harness that power in the classroom; simultaneously, however, I found that my own delight in reading was slowly disappearing, in ways I've described above, in the introduction to *How We Read*. I assume that this was because so much of my daily work was reading, whether for research, class prep, or grading, causing me to lose sight of what it was like to read for pleasure. In the last few months, however, working with Chris Piuma on a podcast about reading called *The Spouter-Inn*, I've begun to rediscover that pleasure in reading through — what else? — reading aloud. Each episode centers on a single book, and while we don't prepare a script, we do sketch out a road map of the themes and — most importantly — the passages we think we might like to talk about, some of which we read aloud.

I've suggested above, in the introduction, that the present volume and *The Spouter-Inn* are, in a sense, twins — both focused on reading, but while *The Spouter-Inn* tries to build enthusiasm and desire for reading on the part of its listeners, *How We Read* instead foregrounds the challenges and pleasures to be found in the act. Both seek to bring out the regenerative, renewing quality of reading, the capacity of one narrative to bring out other stories, for one piece of art to engender another. This quality was beautifully and movingly illustrated when one of our listeners, an artist named Gabriel Liston, commented via Twitter on how he had been listening to *The Spouter-Inn* while finishing his painting *We are not so very broken* (the frontispiece to this essay), an image of an accordion and a book, lit by sunlight. I like to think that this image is part of a cycle, starting with the images that inspired the book Chris and I are reading — whether Gertrude Stein's *Autobiography of Alice B. Toklas* or Melville's *Moby-Dick* — moving to our shared spoken words, reading aloud from the book; to the painter, painting the painting; to the person who responds to Gabriel's work, whether in spoken word or another art form. Reading binds us in a concatenated chain, back into the past of our writers and forward into the future of those readers who will come after us. Reading out loud brings that chain of writers and readers to life.

Jessica Hammer

From When We Read

I read two different ways, so different from one another that you might think I'm describing two different readers.

One way, I dissolve into the text. I'm barely aware of what's on the page; the story comes to life in

FROM WHEN WE READ. *The first words of Tractate Berachot are* m'aimatai korin, *which translates as "from when do we read." In context, the reference is to reciting the* Shema,* *but the opportunity was too good to miss.*

my imagination, but I have no sensation of how it got there. The book becomes invisible, my body disappears, words fly by like telephone poles seen through the window of a speeding train. It's not something I choose so much as something that happens to me. If I need to read slowly, or if I want to appreciate the language, I have to trick myself into reading differently. Reading out loud, for example, will slow me down, even if it's just mumbling the words under my breath. But the moment I forget, I disappear again.

Sometimes I read research papers this way, too, trying to sort through a mass of ideas that might be relevant without getting bogged down. I'll read the title, the abstract, skim the argument, dump it all into my brain and let it work. I might be two or three papers down the line

* SHEMA. *The* Shema *is recited during prayers twice a day, at the morning and evening services. I say it with my daughter every night, after reading her a book and before she gets her hugs and kisses.*

when I realize something seemed interesting and needs a deeper look.

Deeper, that's the other way I read. For research, this means following citation trails to understand what bodies of literature are being referenced, then hunting forward again to see who else is writing about the same things. It might mean stopping to diagram out the procedure for a study to make sure I understand what's happening, or writing angry notes in the margin of a book I disagree with. It could even mean the way I read Choose Your Own Adventure books on my grandmother's old plaid couch in the long hot Maryland summers, using every single finger as a bookmark so I could explore the consequences of choices I hadn't yet made.

It's not an accident that these are the two ways I read, because they're how I was trained to read, and when I say *trained* I mean trained on the ur-text for Orthodox Jews, the Talmud and its accompanying bodies of literature. To read *b'kiyut* meant to move quickly through the text, leaping

NOTES IN THE MARGIN. *These days, I do most of my reading digitally. Annotating on a tablet with a pen is surprisingly satisfying, but I still haven't figured out how to retrieve my notes efficiently. On the other hand, it's not like I went back to my paper-and-pen annotations, either. The important part has always been the process of making them.*

ORTHODOX JEWS. *Although regular Talmud study is most common in Orthodoxy, the Talmud and its interpretive methods are foundational to all denominations. To make claims about Torah*[*] *in the absence of the Talmud is by definition to be outside Rabbinic Judaism.*[†] *Even among Jews who have not studied Talmud themselves, the notion that the Torah cannot be understood in isolation is a cultural touchstone.*

---

* TORAH. *Torah can mean several different things, such as the entire enterprise of Judaic study. In this case, it is intended to highlight the Five Books of Moses, which tend to be a particular yet oddly selective target for self-nominated biblical literalists.* † *Rabbinic Judaism has been the mainstream form of Judaism for more than fifteen hundred years. However, some small communities from other traditions remain.*

from idea to idea, racing to cover as much ground as possible. Reading *b'iyun* meant reading in depth, stopping to look up commentaries, tracing what other people had said about the text back and forth through time.

Growing up in Orthodoxy, Talmud meant adulthood. We began to prepare in sixth grade by studying the Mishna, the second century CE (always CE, never AD) redaction of Oral Law. Mishna was considered easier than Talmud, accessible to the pre-teens we were, but we still sat in front of our densely written Rabbinic Hebrew texts, dictionaries in hand, barely able to stumble through a sentence. In seventh grade, I grew breasts, and spent most of the year hunched forward trying to hide them. I celebrated my *bat mitzvah* in a pink lacy dress from Jessica McClintock. I bought a blue-covered copy of Jastrow's Aramaic dictionary, the one that still sits on my living room shelf today. And, along with the rest of my classmates, I began to study Talmud.

BACK AND FORTH. *If you, for example, are stopping mid-essay to read these footnotes, you are experiencing a taste of what it means to read* b'iyun. *If you want the full experience, I suggest you pause here and spend a week or so researching increasingly loosely related topics, such as identifying every major commentator on the Talmud or defining what "leaping" really means. If you then find it difficult to pick up the thread of this essay, well, you would not be alone.*

NEVER AD. *AD, standing for* Anno Domini, *the year of most-certainly-not-our lord. We were taught that using AD implied a distasteful degree of acceptance that any lord had in fact been born in that year. Worse, it was a profound insult to the millions of Jews murdered in the name of Christian hegemony. Even dating things CE, Common Era, was something of a compromise. After all, we had our own perfectly serviceable calendar.**

---

* PERFECTLY SERVICEABLE. *Well, except for the minor detail of the irregular nineteen year cycle of leap months. And the four different New Years, each of which was used for dating different aspects of Jewish life. And the slow drift away from the solar calendar. But otherwise, perfectly serviceable.*

> IT WAS TAUGHT IN A MISHNA: THESE ARE THE THINGS A PERSON DOES AND ENJOYS THE FRUITS IN THIS WORLD, AND THE PRINCIPAL REMAINS FOR THEM IN THE WORLD TO COME. AND THEY ARE: HONORING YOUR FATHER AND MOTHER, PERFORMING DEEDS OF KINDNESS, AND MAKING PEACE BETWEEN A PERSON AND THEIR FRIEND. AND LEARNING TORAH IS EQUAL TO THEM ALL. *b.Shab.*127a

THE WORLD TO COME. *Judaism is at best ambivalent about the concept of an afterlife. Note that the rhetoric here emphasizes that there are benefits to the listed actions in* this *life, even as it uses the world to come to heighten their importance.*

B.SHAB.127A. *The initial b in this citation tells you that I am referencing the Babylonian Talmud, as opposed to the older but less authoritative Jerusalem Talmud.* Shab *stands for Tractate Shabbat,* 127 *tells you what page to look for, and* a *means it's on the front rather than the back of the page. After that, you're on your own.*

THE DIFFERENCE. *For example, Rashi was a single person; the Tosafot were not.*

TO HOLD A SIYUM. *A* siyum *incorporates a celebratory meal, as do most other Jewish celebrations. If the fast day is minor enough,* the obligation to take part in this meal supersedes the obligation to fast.*

When it came to Talmud, there was a clear hierarchy of ways to read. *B'iyun* was for serious students. If you couldn't explain the difference between Rashi and Tosafot at the drop of a hat, or use the Ein Mishpat to locate the right reference, then what were you even doing in the room? *B'kiyut* had its place, though. If you wanted to hold a *siyum*, the celebration of finishing a major study project, then *b'kiyut* would get you there fast. You might study in honor of someone who had died, or in the name of

---

* MINOR ENOUGH. *I am peculiarly familiar with this loophole because of the Fast of the Firstborn, a fast on the day before Passover that commemorates the sparing of the Jewish firstborns. All firstborn boys are obligated to fast. While there are differing opinions on whether firstborn daughters are also obligated, I figured it was just as easy for me to have my breakfast at the nearest* siyum — *just in case.*

someone who was sick, or because it was a legal way to avoid fasting on certain minor fast days. You could also join the *daf yomi* project, the worldwide community of Jews learning one page of Talmud a day. If you stuck with it, why, you could finish the whole thing in just seven and a half years! Not *b'iyun*, of course. You'd have to keep up with that on your own.

The hierarchy wasn't just of ways to read, though; it was a hierarchy of readers. As a woman, I was an outsider in the world of Talmud. At my school, girls studying Talmud wasn't just normal, it was honorable. While being a brilliant Talmudist wasn't quite as good as being the star of the girls' basketball team, it was close. But outside, things got dicier. Long before I called myself a feminist, I was told that studying Talmud made me one. (It was sadly not intended as a compliment.) I was called unmarriageable, a devastating possibility in a culture centered on home and family. One friend sat me down for a lecture about all the ways that studying Talmud was bad for my reputation. In retrospect I'm sure she meant well, but I never spoke to her again.

THE GIRLS' BASKETBALL TEAM. *Unfortunately, I was both short and uncoordinated.*

AND FROM WHERE IS IT DERIVED THAT OTHERS ARE NOT COMMANDED TO TEACH A WOMAN? AS THE VERSE STATES: "AND YOU SHALL TEACH THEM TO YOUR SONS" (DEUTERONOMY 11:19), WHICH EMPHASIZES: YOUR SONS AND NOT YOUR DAUGHTERS. *b.Kid*.29b

---

In seventh grade, that first year of Talmud, we studied Tractate Berachot, Blessings. At what time did the obligation to pray begin? At dawn, and so the rabbis argued hair-splittingly about different definitions of dawn. Was it at cock-crow, or when you could tell a blue thread from a white, or when the sun became visible over the horizon? Our class picked our way forward slowly, rotating the reader for the text, delving into Rashi. (Rashi always slowed us down because it was written in an entirely different script. Fluency with Rashi script was one of my points of pride.) Little by little, we began to make sense of the rabbis' blend of close textual analysis, wild allegory, and homespun common sense.

Meanwhile, at home, my father and I were studying the obligation to prayer in an entirely different way as we prepared for my *bat mitzvah*. My parents insisted that I be as well-trained and well-prepared for my coming of age as any of the boys around me, if not more so. My mother organized a women's prayer service, where I led the services and read from the Torah, and my father taught me Talmud. We started with a philosophical debate between the two great medieval commentators, Maimonides and Nachmanides. Was prayer defined by form or by intent? Was it a biblical obligation, or merely a rabbinic one? How often did one really have to pray? Why were petitions to God included in prayer, knowing that they are not granted? On each of these issues, Maimonides and Nachmanides took opposing stands. To understand their positions, we danced backward and forward across the centuries. We'd look at a Talmudic precedent, then check a proof-text in the Torah, then leap forward to contemporary halachic analyses. I complained and dragged my feet at the beginning of every study session, but the next day I'd brag to my friends about how much I'd learned. I was studying Talmud in a new and different way.

BAT MITZVAH. *The* bat mitzvah *refers to a girl's coming of age, when she becomes responsible for herself in matters of Jewish law, ritual, and ethics. In the popular imagination, the* bat mitzvah *has become associated with a girl's first participation in Jewish ritual life, such as reading from the Torah for the first time, and with a celebratory party. However, these common activities* mark *a girl becoming* bat mitzvah; *they do not cause it, nor can their absence prevent it.*

> RABBA BAR BAR HANA SAID: WHY ARE MATTERS OF TORAH COMPARED TO FIRE, AS IT IS STATED: "IS NOT MY WORD LIKE FIRE, SAYS THE LORD" (JEREMIAH 23:29)? TO TELL YOU: JUST AS FIRE DOES NOT IGNITE IN A LONE STICK OF WOOD BUT IN A PILE OF KINDLING, SO TOO, MATTERS OF TORAH ARE NOT RETAINED AND UNDERSTOOD PROPERLY BY A LONE SCHOLAR WHO STUDIES BY HIMSELF, BUT ONLY BY A GROUP OF SAGES.
>
> *b.Taan.*7a

After high school, I went to an all-female seminary. We had a morning *b'iyun* Talmud class, divided in groups by skill, but then further divided into study partners, or *chavruta*. We'd sit together with a teacher to discuss a passage or theme, then break into pairs to dig deep into the text ourselves. My Hebrew was good enough that I was placed into the top-level Hebrew-language seminar with the Israeli girls, but not good enough for me to follow most of what the teacher said. Every class, I'd suffer through half-understood lectures, then breathe a sigh of relief. During *chavruta* time I could do what I did best: puzzle through the text, taking notes or drawing diagrams or looking up references if I needed to, feeling the shape of the argument slot into place in my head. "It's so frustrating," I complained late one night to my friend N., who promptly burst into tears. "I can't even follow in English," she sobbed, "and you can *do* this, it's yours, it belongs to you."

IN MY HEAD. *I am exceptionally poor at producing or recalling images in my head.* When I read, I don't see anything being described in any conventional sense. Instead, I experience it as a sort of abstract interlocking that I can feel all through my body. The senses that dominate my reading experience are the kinaesthetic and proprioceptive. This tendency makes my experiences reading Talmud and reading, say, Middlemarch feel surprisingly similar.*

* HEAD. *Until writing this essay, I had no idea this was unusual. Discovering that other people could imagine the faces of their favorite characters without visual aids was a disconcerting surprise.*

That year I studied with a dozen different women. We'd sit opposite one another at narrow tables, heads bent low over our texts, our voices raised in *pilpul*, the chanting tones of Talmudic argument. One was a curly-haired raconteur from Toronto, whose room was always full of visitors after study hours ended. Another, a deceptively serene-seeming blonde who could reliably be provoked into fits of giggles at inopportune moments. A third organized birthday parties and complex arguments with equal, effortless ease. I'd get up before dawn and run three miles through the half-lit Jerusalem streets, then smuggle sweet rolls into the *beit midrash* for the girls who always arrived too late for breakfast. N. was wrong. The Talmud didn't belong to me. It belonged to all of us, together.

BEIT MIDRASH. *The study hall, or more literally the house of learning. In this case, it was a large room with bookshelves on every available wall and long tables down the middle. Each chavruta would stake out their space by stacking books in their preferred spot, usually alongside their shtenders, the olive-wood reading stands that were all the rage. Buying a shtender for your chavruta, and having it personalized with her name and a relevant Torah passage, was considered a profound gesture of friendship.*

RABBI TARFON AND THE ELDERS WERE ONCE RECLINING IN THE UPPER STORY OF NITHZA'S HOUSE, IN LYDDA, WHEN THIS QUESTION WAS RAISED BEFORE THEM: IS STUDY GREATER, OR ACTION? RABBI TARFON ANSWERED, SAYING: "ACTION IS GREATER." RABBI AKIVA ANSWERED SAYING: "STUDY IS GREAT, FOR IT LEADS TO ACTION." THEN THEY ALL ANSWERED AND SAID: "STUDY IS GREATER, FOR IT LEADS TO ACTION." *b.Kid.*40b

---

As much as I loved Talmud, it wasn't enough to help me find a place in Orthodox life. I could study all I wanted, but the pathways that were open to men who loved Talmud weren't open to me. My mother and other Orthodox feminists chose to fight for women's inclusion in Orthodoxy with remarkable courage, scholarship, and persistence. But that was a weight I couldn't carry. I turned away. Instead, I spent a decade practicing a Judaism of refusal. No, I wouldn't break the laws of Shabbat, but I also wouldn't go to synagogue. I wouldn't eat non-kosher food, but I also wouldn't go to a kosher restaurant. No, I wouldn't get married. No, I wouldn't wear skirts. And no, I wouldn't study Talmud.

Instead, I read other things: *The Lord of the Rings*, every year for my birthday; the complete works of Dickens in the frozen months after my father died; role-playing game manuals and psychology research papers and statistics textbooks, for the strange amalgamation of work and play my dissertation had become. I filled the shelves of my tiny apartment three-deep with books, then moved to a larger place and started the process again. I logged every book I read for more than a decade, and wrote capsule reviews to share with friends. Even through the most difficult of times, my reading life was rich, full, joyful.

Talmud was still with me, though, like a ghost in my house. It was in the inflection in my voice when I argued, in the way I traced an idea from text to text, in the Aramaic I'd toss into casual conversations. And slowly, slowly, it came back to me.

SKIRTS. *Or dresses.*

BIRTHDAY. *I started this tradition when I was eight years old and our babysitter lent me his copy of the trilogy. I read them again and again until the spines broke. Then I had to buy him a new set out of my allowance.*

WE WILL RETURN TO YOU, TRACTATE BERACHOT, AND YOU WILL RETURN TO US; OUR MIND IS ON YOU, TRACTATE BERACHOT, AND YOUR MIND IS ON US; WE WILL NOT FORGET YOU, TRACTATE BERACHOT, AND YOU WILL NOT FORGET US — NOT IN THIS WORLD AND NOT IN THE WORLD TO COME.
The *Hadran* Prayer

OUR MIND IS ON YOU. *The word here translated as "mind" is* da'at, *which is also the term for consciousness itself. The reader speaking these words of loss, longing, and renewal to the text they have just read, and imagining the text as able to respond in kind, is glorious and chilling.*

THE HADRAN PRAYER. *The* Hadran *is printed at the end of each tractate of Talmud, with the appropriate tractate name filled in.*

I began again with Berachot, and with the Mishna. This time my husband was my *chavruta*, backing me up from a chunky one-volume English translation while I wrestled with half-forgotten terms. We read *b'kiut*, grappling with how to understand each passage but always moving steadily forward. When we finished Berachot, we thought we might just try to get through one more tractate. Then another, and another. Eventually we realized that if we hurried we could do a *siyum mishna*, a celebration of studying the entire Mishna, to honor our daughter's birth. We raced through the last few chapters just before her due date, saving the last three *mishnayot* to learn the sleep-deprived, achy morning of the naming. As I held my infant daughter in my arms, I recited the ancient prayer of the *Hadran* three times. Then we read the beginning of Berachot aloud, to show that we would not cease to study. I had truly returned to Masechet Berachot, and it had returned to me.

My husband and I are now making our way slowly through the Talmud, starting from Berachot. Once a month, we join friends for a communal study session. Other nights, we learn while our daughter sings to herself in bed. My husband loves the glimpses of historical context, from debates about the value of a nailed sandal to the incorporation of Greek and Latin words. Me, I've been vividly reminded of the odd ways that the Talmud can sometimes be organized. If Rabba bar bar Pappa is mentioned, for example, it might end up with a multipage digression about a bunch of unrelated things he said. We move back and forth between reading *b'kiut* and *b'iyun* fluidly, depending on what we're in the mood for that day. We've talked about doing a *siyum* for our daughter's *bat mitzvah*, but I'm in no rush. We've got a lifetime to study together.

Talmud is as much mine as I choose to make it, and so I claim it. May I someday merit to teach my daughter how to read.

HOW TO READ. *The Steinsaltz edition of the Babylonian Talmud contains both the traditionally formatted text, which you can see in the photograph at the beginning of this essay, and a version that includes English translation. The translation expands the often-cryptic Aramaic text, adding contextual details and making implicit information explicit. However, the English edition includes very minimal commentary and references.*

For the digitally inclined, the Sefaria website contains the full text of the Talmud, along with many commentaries and supporting texts, in both Hebrew and English. It has an excellent internal linking system, including both forward- and back-reference. A free app is also available for both phones and tablets.

Finally, understanding the Talmud requires an enormous amount of context, both about Jewish law and practice, and about the methods for understanding Talmud itself. Steinsaltz's The Essential Talmud *provides a useful introduction.*

Lochin Brouillard

De Vita Lochinis,
or, Commentary on a Life of Reading

I was walking down Spadina Avenue in Toronto, admiring the bright storefronts of Chinatown's restaurants and retailers, when I noticed a T-shirt that proclaimed, "I was born intelligent but education ruined me." This slogan will be no doubt be read differently by another beholder, but on my end, it made me pause and think about the reflections colleagues like Kaitlin and Suzanne have been fostering on how we read and write. Education certainly didn't ruin me — this is what I'll attempt to convey here. Nevertheless, I could relate to the sense of loss, of before and after "education ruined me," which Kaitlin described in her original blog post as she realized that, out of mental saturation caused by the PhD, she couldn't bring herself to read the latest tome of a beloved series she'd been eagerly awaiting for.[1]

Like most, if not all of us, I found my way to history because I loved reading, writing, thinking. Yet on some

---

1 Kaitlin Heller and Suzanne Akbari, "How We Read," *In the Middle* (blog), October 3, 2017, http://www.inthemedievalmiddle.com/2017/10/how-we-read.html.

IMAGE: Years of reading *Astérix* got me used to the footnote-like practice of coming across a Latin name and looking at its modern-day equivalent at the bottom of the panel.
PHOTO: Lochin Brouillard.
DOI: 10.21983/P3.0259.1.07

days, I would do *anything* to get away from reading, writing, thinking, rinsing, and repeating. That things have come to this is particularly painful with regards to reading. Out of the elements of this trinity — reading, writing, thinking — I've always enjoyed the purest, most unwavering relationship with reading. Writing can be exhilarating but equally capricious, demanding, unreliable. Thinking can easily turn into *over*thinking, over-rationalizing, over-intellectualizing. Reading — at least before I came to university — was simple, unadulterated pleasure. It isn't anymore.

Should I blame "academic reading" for ruining my love for reading? I would be lying if I did not admit that it did a little, for the most part because I read fiction much less than I used to. But it would also be inaccurate and ungrateful to fail to recognize how my university training both made me a better reader, and built upon the intuitive joys I've had since I was a child.

I divided this *opusculum* (Latin for "little work") into three sections, two on reading *before* and one on reading *after* my university education.[2] As a historian of the Western Christian Church, and a medievalist working with hagiography (that is, saints' Lives), I found this before/after motif meaningful because it implies a critical juncture, an episode of conversion which changes everything and acts as a key for making intelligible what falls on either temporal side of it. Being a scholar in the humanities is construed — for better or worse — as an ascetic pursuit, a calling, a vocation, perhaps not so different from the way the people I study entered the religious life. In writing this essay, I used my academic conversion as the pivot through

---

[2] The term *opusculum* is often used by medieval writers as part of a humility *topos* of which I, a modest, insignificant grad student, am availing myself.

which I read my own past, looking for clues for what came later. I turned to my own experiences with a "typological" outlook, to borrow the language of exegesis, and tried to pinpoint which signs prefigured my current circumstances as a medieval historian.³

Hagiography offers different models of sanctity, with saints who struggle and lose their way only to walk the straight and narrow path later in life, while other ones, the *pueri senes* (Latin for "old boys") who read Scriptures while the average children run and play, are set on a trajectory towards eternal salvation from their time in their mother's womb.⁴ The narrative I construct about myself conforms to this latter pattern, probably because my historiographical tendencies lean towards continuity rather than dramatic breaks. (It's apparently a gendered characteristic: female saints are less prone to rupture than their male counterparts.⁵)

---

3 In medieval studies, exegesis mainly refers to the practice of biblical commentary. A typological reading connects events, figures, statements or symbols from the Hebrew Bible (or Old Testament) with those of the New Testament.

4 The authors of medieval saints' Lives might represent their saints as so precocious that they could be said to be "old" (*senes*) though they are only "boys" (*pueri*). Like Christ at the Temple, these prematurely wise children discuss the Scriptures and are turned towards the higher things.

5 Julia H. Smith found that female saints are bound to a familial setting in Carolingian hagiography while Caroline Walker Bynum observed that, on account of their lack of control over their property and marital status, late-medieval religious women were less prone to dramatic conversions and to breaking away from their kin, than religious men. See Smith, "The Problem of Female Sanctity in Carolingian Europe, c. 780–920," *Past and Present* 146 (1995): 25–28; and Bynum, *Holy Feast and Holy Fast: The Religious Significance of Food to Medieval Women* (Berkeley: University of California Press, 1988), 24–25.

Narrative, repetition and serial reading

I have always been a compulsive reader. My parents like to recount that, before I had learnt to read myself, they would read me bed time stories every night, and inevitably, once they reached the end of the book, the first word that came out from my mouth was *"Encore!"* My childhood was spent reading: at the dinner table, in the car, during long baths, at school when I was done with the assignments. Some habits die hard: I still pick up the shampoo bottle to have something to read in the shower.

Driven by the same impulse that compelled me to ask my parents to tell me a story over and over, I began to read and re-read books again and again. There were *bandes-dessinées* like my father's tattered Astérix collection to which I returned tirelessly. I have Astérix to thank for my capacity to immediately recognize Latin place names like *Lugdunum* (modern-day Lyon) or *Massilia* (modern-day Marseille). Most of all, I drew this deep pleasure from knowing and anticipating all the jokes and their punch-lines, while still noticing, upon another reading, new visual details or word plays.

The illustrated Bible I received for my first communion was also a constant in the rotating pile of books next to my bed. Being from semi-secular francophone Québec, I grew up in a non-practicing, culturally Catholic environment. This mostly entailed going through the liturgical and sacramental milestones but not spending much time on the theological intricacies my parents' generation had learnt in catechism class. At school, we were taught (and were asked to draw with our array of felt pens) the moral lessons of the New Testament. When I came home, it was the stories of the Hebrew Bible I found most riveting, if more difficult to understand. Like the tales of Greek or Egyptian mythology I adored, the narratives of Cain and Abel or King Solomon depicted all manners of human behavior: bravery, endurance, sacrifice, violence, jealousy... A lot of it seemed cruel, unfair, or outright distressing to my eight-year-old self — why is it better to offer meat than the fruits of the harvest to God? How could David go from being the courageous boy who had defeated Goliath to a monarch who stole his soldier's wife and sent him to his death? — when it did not feel mysterious and foreign. Beyond this, it gave me respect, even reverence for texts which feel impenetrable at first, texts which survived for thousands of years and hold an ancient wisdom that can be unlocked with a labor of love.

Like the monks and nuns I study today, I was unwittingly engaging in a light form of *ruminatio*, reading and re-reading the same matter, absorbing it until it had been shelved in the reference section of my mental library.[6] I suspect that I also relished in the intimacy and the omniscience that grows out of repetition. The philosopher Louis Mink pointed out that the reader of history is a reader who knows how the story ends, and can therefore conceive temporal succession "in both directions at once, and then time is no longer the river which bears us along but the

---

6 In medieval monastic literature, *ruminatio* is a term "borrowed from eating, from digestion, and from the particular form of digestion belonging to ruminants." It refers to the twin practice of meditation and reading: "To meditate is to attach oneself closely to the sentence being recited and weigh all its words in order to sound the depths of their full meaning. It means assimilating the content of a text by means of a kind of mastication which releases its full flavor." Jean Leclercq, *The Love of Learning and The Desire for God: A Study of Monastic Culture*, trans. Catharine Misrahi, 3rd ed. (New York: Fordham University Press, 1985), 73.

river in an aerial view, upstream and downstream seen in a single survey."[7] This quality of knowing how the story ends at times makes certain works of historical fiction too unbearable for me to watch. I had to stop a television series on the Second World War, which covers about a year of the war per season, because I could not handle the increasing persecution of the Jewish characters... and we were only in 1942! In less emotionally harrowing cases, I enjoyed the sense of foreboding and the tragic irony that imbue a narrative whose end I know in advance. There's a definite thrill to novelty and discovery, but many of the works that have stayed with me are those I've re-read or re-watched, armed with the power of hindsight.

A close cousin to this repetitive reading is what I would call serial reading, which is best epitomized by my systematic devouring of Agatha Christie's crime novels between the age of ten and twelve. I believe that I appreciated their form: there was always a detective, a crime, a number of suspects, an investigation, plot twists, and a grand reveal. It was fun to add up the clues and measure my hunches against Hercule Poirot's exposition at the end of the book. More than this, I was learning the laws of a genre, the narrative economy that dictates that if a novel counts 250 pages and a suspect is arrested on page 110, they're probably not the actual culprit but a red herring the author is throwing at you before they lay their cards on the table. Like Astérix or the Bible, Agatha Christie's novels brought together freshness and familiarity, blended with the delights of being clever and being right.

In my research, I might have gravitated towards hagiographical sources for the same reason that I liked reading

---

7 Louis Mink, "History and Fiction as Modes of Comprehension," *New Literary History* 1 (1970): 554–55.

Agatha Christie's detective fiction. Scholars of hagiographical literature have highlighted its conservative character, if not in terms of production than in terms of edition. The same saints and the same references tend to predominate, no matter the century.[8] Saints' Lives themselves are redundant and rarely deviate from their well-trodden path. Yet, *vitae*, like Agatha Christie's novels, could almost be considered an acquired taste, a literature that keeps on giving the more and the better you become acquainted with it. Having read a handful of major works is not enough to truly get the feel for it. You need to have gone through dozens of them to arrive at the joy and the ability of identifying common tropes *and* of spotting idiosyncrasies.

Comprehensive reading, the canon, and the bibliographical impulse

As a scholar and as an individual, I am keen on systems and patterns, organization and structure. I find it satisfying to enter a field, get acquainted with its theoretical and methodological underpinnings, and assimilate a well-defined body of knowledge. It's important but also pleasurable and empowering for me to learn to determine authoritative sources, collect my own data, and compare it to what others have found. In my day-to-day, this translates into

---

8   While thousands of saints' Lives were composed in the medieval period, only a fraction of these reached a wide audience. The saints whose Lives were assembled by editors for a collection or an anthology were often the same usual suspects. Monique Goullet, *Écritures et réécritures : Essai sur les réécritures de Vies de saints dans l'Occident latin médiéval (VIIIe-XIIIe s.)* (Turnhout: Brepols 2005), 13–14.

keeping lists of all kinds (board games, ciders, favorite songs). I rarely chance upon things: I consult lists on the top 10 bibimbaps in Toronto or I follow the Cannes film festival for movie recommendations. Building a bibliography or establishing a framework for grasping a specific topic are not just research skills: they're concrete life skills.

Again, it is easy to trace back these traits to my childhood. I always had an interest in fictional world-building: between the age of eight and twelve years old, I went through a *Star Wars*, followed by a *Lord of the Rings*, and a *Harry Potter* phase. Then just as now, I was emotionally invested in the characters and the story arc, but I also immersed myself in what is referred to by fans as the "lore." It didn't matter that it wasn't "real" — I *had* to know everything. Even before this, I remember being fond of a book based on the movie *The Pagemaster*, in which Macaulay Culkin travels to a fantasy world populated with characters from fairy tales and horror and adventure classics. It was a *Where's Waldo* type of book, divided by genres, which asked its readers to identify well-known stories based on key visual details. I was not overly interested in the *Where's Waldo* exercise. Instead I flipped to the last pages of the book which provided a summary of each story, presented in bland, encyclopedic columns. I was utterly fascinated by this repository of knowledge which allowed me to learn about all these essential books in a couple of sentences.

I didn't know it then, but *The Pagemaster* served as a primer for the works one might expect to encounter in popular culture or in English courses on the "Western tradition." Decades later, I would no doubt go back to *The Pagemaster*'s overwhelmingly male, Western-centric selection with a critical eye. I have become a firm believer in the idea that the "traditional canon" of any area or discipline should be questioned, opened up, and diversified. Some think that we should do away with canons entirely — I'm not one of them. Perhaps because of the way in which my brain functions, both in my research and my teaching, I see the use of having canons as starting points from which we can depart.

Besides this attachment for mastering canons, I've long had a bibliographical itch, which ties in with my Agatha Christie obsession. Indeed, as I kept on reading Christie's works, I eventually felt the need to keep track of my progression, and thus created a sheet, which recorded the title of the book, the detective featured in it, my review (out of five stars), and additional comments. Looking back, I am surprised — but maybe shouldn't be — that a child of eleven found this an appropriate use of their time. Why did I do this? This was not part of a school project. I might have showed it to my parents since I share everything with them, but I don't recall supplying it to my friends. As far as I can tell, this was simply something I did for my own entertainment.

This impulse of drawing lists and exploring the canon was consummated at around the same period. Before the days of Wikipedia, my family owned the Encarta encyclopedia on CD-ROM which I spent hours perusing. Again, the hopeless nerd I was gathered and typed for fun short lists of the "most famous Russian authors," the "most famous French authors," etc. I then dutifully went to the public library to pick up *Crime and Punishment* or *Lolita*, which I proceeded to read at the "nymphet" age described by Humbert Humbert. Truth be told, I abandoned many of these great classics, which passed quite over the head of the ambitious young reader I was. Nonetheless, I am glad that it even occurred to me to try, and that I saw some worth in difficult readings.

Becoming a better reader

Like Kaitlin and Suzanne, I remember a point during my undergraduate degree when I realized that my studies had spoiled reading. Instead of simply enjoying the novel in my hands, I was scanning the page, looking for the "most relevant information" or the "overarching point" to each paragraph. Unmitigated, freeing pleasure came back after some time spent in the arms of a real page-turner, but it remained jarring to acknowledge that something which used to be so natural had been tainted by an imperative for efficiency.

I maintain though that university did not ruin reading for me. Rather, it changed the way I interact with a text. I credit Nancy Partner, my mentor at McGill University, for this. In a classroom, I am usually very engaged, a second away from raising my hand to speak my mind. Nancy Partner's classes were a distinct experience for me, closer to the one that medical students in the past would have had, as they huddled together to observe their professor slicing a body open and giving a lecture on anatomy. This is because no one dissects a text like Nancy Partner. She possesses an acuity, a precision, an insightfulness into the ways in which narrative and the human mind work that I have never witnessed in anybody else. I would sit in silent awe, frantically recording every observation being pronounced, and bristle at those who interrupted the master class.

The most memorable reading exercise she assigned the class consisted in locating, organizing, and commenting on all the instances of theft, writing, or food in Galbert of Bruges' chronicle on the murder of Count Charles the Good in Flanders in 1127. That simple technique of isolating one thematic element in a text was a revelation, something that I have used ever since, and have passed on to my own students. Before Nancy Partner, I would not have been able to articulate strategies for pulling apart, zooming in, and zooming out on bits and pieces of a text like I learned during my BA.

Nancy's seminars also made me a better reader because they introduced me to — or more accurately, made me fall in love with — medieval texts. Like any premodern texts, medieval texts can baffle us because they were not meant for us: they defy the narrative logic we are used to; they jump from one topic to the next in flabbergasting bouts of parataxis; they treat bizarre events in a matter-of-fact manner or explain them in ways that appear completely outlandish. University taught me to be a "resisting reader" who *reads against* texts, but it also taught me to read texts who, by their very nature, resist *me*.

Since these early steps in medieval studies, it has been rewarding to close the gap produced by the alterity of the premodern text, by learning everyday a little more about medieval society, culture, and thought. Now, when I plunge into eleventh-century monastic chronicles, I am on board with my brothers or sisters. I understand why it's absolutely outrageous that a certain bishop refused to confirm the election of an abbot, or what a glorious event it is when the Pope himself consecrates a newly built church! Granted, I am still bewildered and greatly amused by the quirks and wonders of medieval texts...Who could keep a straight face when reading about, *mirabile dictu*, flesh-eating mice sailing waters atop the rinds of pomegranates?[9]

I am constantly moved too by the closeness I have developed for the often anonymous authors of my medieval sources. I recall breaking down into tears as I came upon Henry of Huntingdon's address to the reader at the end of his twelfth-century *Historia Anglorum*:

> Now I speak to you who will be living in the third millennium, around the 135th year. Consider us, who at this moment seem to be renowned, because, miserable creatures, we think highly of ourselves. Reflect, I say, on what has become of us.... I, who will already be dust by your time, have made mention of you in this book, so long before you are to be born, so that if — as my soul strongly desires — it shall come

---

9 "I have heard a man of the highest veracity telling how one of the emperor [Henry IV]'s adversaries... was leaning back one day as he sat at dinner, when he was suddenly densely beset by a wall of mice that he had no means of escape.... I am the less disposed to think that remarkable, because it is a known fact that in Asia, if anyone has been bitten by a leopard, an army of mice at once gathers to make water on the wounded man.... The man who told me this had seen the victim of such an attack who, in despair of surviving on land, had put out to sea and cast anchor. Without delay, ever so many mice sailed after him, enclosed, believe it or not, in the rinds of pomegranates of which they had eaten the flesh." William of Malmesbury, *The History of the English Kings*, ed. and trans. R.A.B. Mynors, Rodney M. Thomson, and Michael Winterbottom (Oxford: Clarendon Press, 1998), 525.

> about that this book comes into your hands, I
> beg you, in the incomprehensible mercy of God,
> to pray for me, poor wretch.[10]

There's an unfathomable poignancy about reading the existential anxieties of a man who lived centuries ago, and feeling kinship and sympathy for him across the vastness of time. The child I was would be ecstatic to learn that she would later turn these passions for grappling with challenging texts and writing about them into a full-time occupation. It is a privilege and a pleasure I try to honor as much as I can.

---

10 Henry of Huntingdon, *The History of the English People, 1000–1154*, trans. Diana Greenaway (Oxford: Oxford University Press, 1996), 119.

Chris Piuma

How I Read

Imagine me as a two-year-old. My parents have told me that, even at two, I could read. There's a story that once, at a hotel, strangers noticed me reading, and they were impressed and startled. Maybe scared? I don't know. I don't remember any of this. I don't remember how I read. I also don't remember what it was like to be unable to read. I don't remember before and after reading. Was there a moment of epiphany, when the written word transformed from arbitrary scratches into legible text? When the concept of reading itself, as a possibility, finally occurred to me? What would that even feel like?

Imagine me at seven. I am walking home from elementary school along tree-lined suburban streets. On the six-block walk home (it's the 1980s; I'm allowed to walk home on my own) my nose is buried in a library book. Probably an *Encyclopedia Brown* book. Leroy "Encyclopedia" Brown, Boy Detective, is the star of a seemingly infinite series of books. Apparently there were maybe sixteen of them when I was seven? I remember hundreds. Each *Encyclopedia Brown*

IMAGE: The author as a frustrated young reader. PHOTO: Unknown.

book contains several short stories in which the boy detective is presented with mysteries that test his wits. And the reader's wits: The solution to each mystery is held off, printed in the back of the book, and you, the reader, are told that you have the same clues that Encyclopedia Brown had in order to solve the mystery. Had you figured it out? Were you as clever as Encyclopedia Brown?

You were not. Or, you rarely were. Or, I rarely was. Reading the *Encyclopedia Brown* books now, the mysteries are a bit crap. They require arcane knowledge, misguided cultural assumptions, and an ability to read the author's mind. None of that mattered to me then. The books felt clever. Encyclopedia Brown seemed clever. The books felt like a master class in learning how to be a clever detective. They weren't, but they felt that way. They blurred the lines between the character and the reader. Especially if you reread the stories. The second time through, you were much more clever than Encyclopedia Brown, Boy Detective. You could solve the mystery even before you had all the evidence. You were so clever, you might as well be psychic. You might as well have magic powers. You no longer had to *imagine* yourself with magic powers: This was the non-fictional you, going about your day, being asked questions by a book, and able to answer them with preternatural ability.

—§—

Imagine me at thirteen. I go to school in Manhattan, and have the freedom to go wherever I wanted on my lunch breaks. I am given an allowance for lunch money, and I have figured out the most affordable lunch that would sustain me (a bagel and cream cheese, $0.99) so I can spend the rest of my money on sci-fi and fantasy novels, which I devour.

Nowadays I wonder: What did I do with my body while I read? I would read in bed for hours at a stretch. This shouldn't be so physically demanding, but I have difficulty with it today. And yet I can watch YouTube videos or play video games or work on my laptop in bed for as long as I'd like. But reading? Reading now seems to require some sort of physical constraint, like being trapped in a plane or on a subway car. Otherwise, my body gets antsy.

Imagine me at eighteen. I am in college. I have gone to college mostly because it's the path of least resistance. I tell myself that I'm going to be a writer. I'm majoring in creative writing at a school that doesn't really offer that as a major — but I figure no one needs to go to university for creative writing. Surely the best way to become a writer is to write a lot.

I do not write a lot. I skip class a lot. I park myself in the library, reading the secondary literature about James Joyce. I had tried to read *Ulysses* when I had first heard its reputation as a challenging masterpiece, but I was maybe fourteen years old then, and despite my self-assurance, I didn't get very far. I don't get very far this time either. (I still haven't read it cover to cover.) But I read a lot of books *about* Joyce.

And then I get distracted from *Ulysses* by discovering *Finnegans Wake*. Talk about your challenging masterpieces! *Finnegans Wake* is a massive novel with barely a wisp of plot. It is constructed out of a dense web of multilingual puns, puns so deep and resonant that any sentence can elicit pages and pages of annotations and conjectures. A book so eager to be glossed that, as Joyce said, "it will keep the professors busy for centuries."[1]

I lose a year trying to read *Finnegans Wake*. I am dating someone who lives across town from me, and as I take the two-hour subway ride to visit him each weekend, I slowly read the *Wake*, filing the margins with my own annotations and conjectures. I get through about a page and a half each way. When I arrive, I'm dizzy, and it is jarring to reintegrate to standard English. But each week I chip away at it, working towards that moment when the language will become clear and legible, when I will be able to read the text as confidently as the scholars who comment on it, when I too will be fluent and sure of its meaning. When I will be able to read it like any other text.

An epiphany finally happens, but it is not the one I expect. *Finnegans Wake* does not become legible as a communicative code, as a hyperdetermined text that expertly weaves its puns and allusions into a single coherent thrust of meaning, something solved by the scholars, a mystery whose solution is knowable through research and rereading. No. Instead, I realize, the pleasure lies in how the text is overdetermined, how so much is woven into each word and sentence and character and structure that it manages to simultaneously resist meaning and suggest meaning, in a commodius vicus of recirculation.

Eventually I will wonder if you can read any text like this.

---

[1] Quoted in Richard Ellmann, *James Joyce*, 2nd ed. (Oxford: Oxford University Press, 1982), 521.

HOW I READ

— § —

Keep imagining me at eighteen. I take a compulsory composition class. We sometimes start the class with a minute or two of unstructured freewriting, after which those who are so moved are invited to read their freewriting aloud. One day, I have nothing on my mind, and so I write an arbitrary noun. Because that is the trick, right? Just start making marks, and eventually you'll decide upon something. So I write another arbitrary noun. Peanut. Branch. Pebble. Argentina. Brake. Spine. Terrier. Switch. Sailboat. Neptune. The game, I realize as I play it, is to keep coming up with nouns without pausing, but to try to have each noun unrelated to the nouns near it. It's trickier than you might think. It also turns out to be more mentally stimulating than having something to write about. It's a rush.

I offer to read my text aloud, at least some of it. Poster. Packet. Tarmac. Insert. Bookmark. Can. Balustrade. Transmission. *Disparu*. Whelk. And after I read for a bit, the instructor says: "Have you ever read any Ann Lauterbach? She's a language poet..."

She gives me a quick bibliography, and I rush off to the library. It's an unexpected treasure trove. So many weird poets, doing so many interesting things with language, with such unlikely theoretical justification! Language poetry emerged in the US in the late 1970s at the juncture of theory, activism, and experimental poetry, and the dozen or so people involved produced poetry, manifestos, criticism, and yet more theory. None of it quite convinces me that avoiding normative signification will overthrow capitalism, but the poetry gets me excited anyway. It offers so many possibilities for how else language might work. Or, no, it uses language to get at the dusty corners of my mind. It shakes out the rugs.

How do you get at what's going on inside you that your well-worn paths of communicative language can't or won't get at? The experience, the emotion, the sensation, the pleasure? You have to be indirect. You rattle things around. How do you describe what is uncovered? Well, you probably can't. That's fine. Language, I love you, you permeate me — but you don't own me.

—§—

Imagine me at twenty-five. I've been working in office jobs for a few years. I know this because my upper back hurts. The jobs are designed to keep you at a desk for far more hours than are needed to get your work done. But by now I've been on the internet for a few years, and the internet is filled with people, people you can trade words with, through email or forums. And it's filled with wonders. People are putting all sorts of different types of writing, from an increasing variety of perspectives, online. I spend my days sampling a little of everything.

—§—

Imagine me at thirty-two. I am too restless at office jobs. All that sitting around, doing anything but the job. What should I do instead? I go back to school to finish my long-abandoned bachelor's. Should I study graphic design? It seems impractical. Then one day at the bookstore, I pick up a used French novel by an author I love, but who I have always read in translation. Suddenly I am using my rusty, rusty French reading skills, and suddenly I remember the delights of reading in a language you barely understand. Of studying a new language. I decide to study Greek and Latin, to undertake a Classics minor. But my Latin instructor is a medievalist, and he brings us a few medieval texts to read. And they are astonishing! They break the rules of Classical Latin, rules which the textbook pretends are inviolable. And they are broken in such curious ways, sometimes mixing in vernacular languages (French, English . . .), sometimes just throwing language at the wall to see what will stick.

It would be a bit much to say that Medieval Latin is, to Classical Latin, what Joycean English is to standard English — but maybe only a bit? These medieval writers were not high modernists, and their technologies of writing were different (but then again, considering the state of the *Wake*'s manuscripts and the impossibility of editing them, that comparison could be teased out more . . .). But even if the texts were constructed with very different mindsets, they could, to the right reader (e.g., me), be very resonant. There was an affinity here. At the very least, these were texts that certain readers — we who love to be astonished by writing that expands the possibility-space of language — ought to know about.

I would not go to grad school intending to write my dissertation about that anachronistic similarity in textual pleasure and possibility, but that's the topic I ended up on. I didn't finish that dissertation, though. These paragraphs are all that remains.

But for me at thirty-two, the other temptation to enter academia is that it will be an excuse to discover, to read, and to buy weird books. Small books of manuscript abbreviations; concordances; recondite dictionaries; scholarly editions of texts with cryptic apparatuses; hyperfocused studies of a text, or an aspect of a text; replicas of manuscripts; catalogues of manuscripts, which, in the right hands, could be read like an Agatha Christie. The most exciting scholarly publications push what it means to be a book, what the appropriate form for a book to take is. Entering academia would be license to indulge in new and unpopular modes of reading.

—§—

Imagine me in grad school. The graph of my reading habits over the course of my time in grad school looks like the boa constrictor eating the elephant in *Le Petit Prince*: my reading ramps up, plateaus, and then collapses.

    I collapse with it.

—§—

I write this in April 2018, a few years after leaving grad school. It is a time when Facebook still exists. Oh look: Someone is complaining about their job. Someone wishes happy birthday to distant relatives (twins). Someone's travel plans have been upended. Someone has a new haircut. A study shows that most people can't pick a lowercase "g" out of a line up. Someone has existential dread. Someone is hoping their house will sell soon. Someone complains about local politics. Someone wishes for a different life, but feels they can't achieve it. Someone complains about Facebook. Someone complains about local politics. Someone complains about police murdering a civilian. Someone is raising money for a good cause. Someone crowdsources the answer to a nerdy question. Someone posts a band's derisible PR photo. Someone mourns a friend's death. Someone posts an album they're enjoying. Someone complains about the weather. Someone is justifying the humanities. Someone has organized women to take back a local scene that had been savaged by toxic masculinity. Someone's child has turned seventeen. Someone has taken a selfie. Someone crowdsources technical help. Someone crowdsources a pick-me-up. Someone is selling a keyboard. Someone posts an article about a senate race. Someone recounts a conversation they overheard. Someone links to a video of recent activism. Someone quotes a tv show. Someone is reminded of their childhood in the USSR. Someone shares a meme that mocks MRAs. Someone posts a funny picture of animals. Someone links to an article about the relevance of classical literature to today's politics. Someone links to a humorous article. Someone shares a cute animal video. Someone shares a nineteenth-century painting. Someone shares a cute animal photo. Someone has opinions about fashion. Someone posts an article about the effects of climate change. Someone links to a humorous article. Someone shares a fierce animal photo. Someone links to an article about a recent school shooting. Someone posts about local politics. Someone posts a cute animal photo. Someone recounts a conversation they overheard. Someone posts a photo of food. Someone posts a photo of their friend's new book. Someone shares a photo from a student protest. Someone posts a meme about the political response to a recent school shooting. Someone posts a song they like. Someone quotes a TV show.

Someone shares a cartoon about the life stages of an avid reader and book buyer. Stage six is "no books" — a chasm in the midst of a reader's life, after a steep fall, with an arduous climb out of it.

—§—

Imagine me at forty-two. Hi. This is me today. I am trying to climb out of the pit of no reading. I am starting over. And so I recently read some fantasy books, Terry Pratchett's *Tiffany Aching* series. They're marketed to young readers, but they may be even better for adult readers? Tiffany Aching is a young girl who will learn to be a witch. While she has access to magic, most of her power stems from being willing to do jobs others won't — and being able to think about her thinking. Metacognition is a more useful and magical skill than anything Encyclopedia Brown offered.

The books are delightful and keep me away from the dreary world for a while, but I have a secret. I have not been reading the writing I love best, the kind of writing that pushes at language: I have not been reading poetry. I have only just left behind that dissertation about the pleasures of writing that expands and reconfigures language in the ways I've tried to hint at, which I was pleasantly surprised to find in a few medieval texts. But I spent so many years trying to write it into ordinary communicative language. Language like the language in most of this essay, but even more formal. And of course I was spending my time reading up on a body of academic writing that was, for the most part, written in standard academic prose. The prose that made up the conversation that I was trying to enter into. And I am not saying that the writing was bad — but I was drowning in it. I was spending a lot of time thinking about it and trying to reckon with it. It was weighing me down, like a pair of concrete boots. And the writing that I had so often taken refuge in, that I had found the pleasures of escape in? Well, I was wearing the concrete boots in order to better think and write about that writing. They had become all too connected.

I have not stopped buying books of weird poetry. But they remain in piles on my to-read shelf. This essay was going to be my excuse to read through them and try to talk about them, but I'm still not ready to read them, never mind figure out how to talk about them.

Imagine me someday figuring this out — but not today.

```
E L Y U C M F K F I M F O C G
U X X M Z G F W P F X M H F T
B X F S A E I F N A F U V P X
H U J U J R P Q J N R G S G Q
J T X P O E G U Z O G Y L X K
F B L V A D N I P I R U E C E
S K S O N T B R N T Z S J D G
D E Z I T X N K B A I T L O Q
F E D Y O K U M X T L B E O C
J B L W V C W S I O X I D B W
V U M B U H N Z J N K Y A D X
I T H Q A A O C H N Y O A P K
K O J P S S Y Q U A D G J W L
I B H U F B I I D L I D L E V
G A D R N U D D R O S B R L D
J C U Y I G Y D E F A Y W B W
E K A W S J S T D S B K K X B
W W A E S L L N A V I U L N R
H A B C D P E W E P L V O Z E
U R I G W R X X R Q I G G L C
R D O B C O I L I C T Y M T I
B S S K T Q C V F A Y D N T E
V I P Y C L N Y A L L D J B V
A R G M P Z P R I V I L E G E
U C U X D P D H U F U J O A U
```

Stephanie Bahr

How I Read, a History;
or, "San Francisco Banking
Contains No Trans Fats"

In the fall of 2007, I went to a café in The Mission district to bang my head against the assigned readings for my graduate-level introduction to literary theory. As I encountered Stanley Fish's reader-response theory for the first time, I noticed a rather clever bit of advertising over the coffeeshop's ATM: "San Francisco Banking Contains No Trans Fats." Of course, I chuckled to myself, since banking — at SF Bank or elsewhere — will never contain any trans fats. Nor any calories neither! It seemed an apt bit of satirical advertising for a place so full of health-conscious preachers and diet-craze converts. Amused, I continued my reading.

As I stopped to read the fine print on my way out of the café, however, I was momentarily bewildered to find discussions of snickerdoodles, delivery, and gluten-free or vegan options. "San Francisco Baking Contains No Trans Fats." I chuckled to myself again. It was simply one of my perennial misreadings, an often entertaining fact of life. And it occurred to me then that even reader-response theory wasn't well equipped to deal with the quirks of my brain, a constant factory of lexical and scribal error that would put Adam Scryvain to shame. These misreadings are legindary in my family, a frequent source of in-jokes. As a teenager, I asked my brother for a cup of Twiggins and, faced with his utter confusion, insisted with considerable vehemence that it was the brand of tea our parents bought. Even presented with the packaging as evidence, it still looked like Twiggins to me until I slowed down and named each letter to myself aloud in sequence: T-w-i-n-i-n-g-s. (My family now regularly calls tea Twiggins.)

Eventually, I catch most of these mistakes, usually quiet quickly because the misread word makes no sense in context. Likewise when I jump to the wrong line of text, as I often do, the tracking error mars the sense of the passage and I soon realize it. But going back to correct these misreadings takes time, so when asked "how I read," the first word that comes to mind is lowly. Very slowly. A few years ago in a job placement workshop, we were all instructed to bring a draft of our job letters for peer editing and everyone read them on the spot, no preparation possible. When our faculty workshop leader said, "It looks like everyone's about done," I was still less than half looks like everyone's way through the first page of a two-page letter that everyone else had finished. I gave *lots* of feedback on how everyone opened their letters; I didn't want to slow the event down by admitting how far behind I was. More recently, at the British Library's exhibit on the Anglo-Saxons last week, I found myself the object of constant antipathy when I took the time I needed to read the curator's notes in front of a manuscript before moving aside. I eventually gave up on reading the notes at all since the font was small, the location awkward, and reading at my usual pace brought about such resentment. And, if I'm being honest, part of me was simply embarrassed by the very public reminder of how slowly I read, something I tend to forget until there's an external sign. (Or rather, what I forget is that some people — most people, particularly academics — tend to read with absurd, dizzying speed the likes of which I cannot imagine. Slow, after all, is always relative).

As a grad student at UC Berkeley, I discovered that it was becoming ok to admit that writing is hard and that there is no one way to write. This is all to the good! But what I never heard anyone talk about was the possibility that *reading* is hard. Not just a particular text or theorist or writer, but the very mechanics of reading. (Perhaps they didn't find it hard; perhaps they didn't feel able to say so.) For me, reading is hard — harder than writing. I tire easily. I make mistakes. I must go very slowly.

"Slow" is the word my first grade teacher used to describe me. Not the pace at which I did things, but *me*. I was failing first grade and she was eager to reassure my parents that I wasn't lazy or badly behaved; I was trying, but I was "slow." And I was not the type of kid who would be going to college. This conversation precipitated my first round of diagnostic testing. (Since the first grade, I have had over forty-seven hours of testing.) These tests have round of diagnostic testing. (Since the have revealed, on three separate occasions, that I have impaired visual perception and processing, particularly in sequencing, spatial/visual relations, perceptual organization, processing speed, and visual and working memory.[1] The now outmoded (but familiar) term for many of my neurological quirks is "dyslexia"; the broader, more current diagnostic term is "learning disability." (Though as I joke to my students, I'm quite good at *learning* — I just struggle with certain discrete cognitive functions.) After my diagnosis, I got additional tutoring from a learning specialist who taught me adaptive techniques tailored to the quirks of my brain and diagnosis. Moreover, I fell under the protection of the Americans with Disabilities Act, passed the same year I was first diagnosed. As a result, I was legally entitled to double time on all of my testing, crucial accommodation for someone whose reading speed is in the third percentile.[2]

My initial diagnosis was the most life-altering event I've ever experienced and is a constant, powerful reminder of my privilege. These potentially life-changing tests are time consuming, must be administered by a licensed learning psychologist, and are rarely covered by health insurance. And as an upper-middle-class white child with well-educated parents, my struggles were also more likely to be favorably interpreted by my teachers; that I might not be "cut out for" college was surprising rather than expected. If I had been born into the adverse circumstances of many

---

[1] I find the precision of my diagnostic paperwork oddly comforting. When I was an undergraduate, a psychology major told me that if a neurotypical person and I both read with electrodes on our heads, different parts of our brains would light up. At eighteen, this felt reassuringly concrete to me. Biological. Not abstract or subjective. Certainly not *fictional* — as the high school teacher I idolized once told me: "Learning disabilities aren't real. It's a bogus diagnosis purchased by wealthy parents to soothe their bruised egos about their underperforming kids."

[2] Though one of my teachers found this (legally required) accommodation too "inconvenient" and the school refused to intervene. This happens all too frequently despite the ADA.

of my students and gone undiagnosed and unaccommodated, I doubt I could have graduated from high school, let alone gone to college or received a PhD. My life and even my sense of self would likely be so different it's hard to imagine. Would books and reading still inspire the visceral sense of loathing and humiliation I remember from childhood? Might I think of myself not as a slow reader, but merely "slow"?

As a child, pages of text all looked like a big word hunt puzzle to me. So I read with three popsickle word hunt puzzle sticks: one above the line one below the line, and one to the left of my focus word. The mechanics of all these moving parts was a bit complicated and obviously slow. In sixth grade, I finally dropped from three to two, and then from two to one. As a young teen, reading without any physical tool became a point of pride, but as a more confident adult I'm often very tactile with my books, running my finger across the line as I read or covering part of the text with a sheet of paper, an envelope, or pencil. The fewer lines and words in sight, the less likely I am to jump. When I'm working on a digital text, I make the text as jump large as possible for the same reason. I read Word documents on a 27-inch screen at 300% so there are only about 200 words and 14 lines in view at any time. The fewer words and lines I have to contend with, the fewer tracking errors I'll make; the fewer tracking errors I make, the more efficiently I get through a text and the less frustrated I become.

(While reading this piece, you may have experienced a similar frustration at finding words in the wrong places or words don't make sense in context. Those aren't typos or typesetting errors; they're an attempt to approximate my reading experience for you.)

I also use a wonderful web browser plug-in called Beeline Reader, designed to reduce tracking errors for people with various neurological quirks like mine. It color codes from left to right, changing colors as demonstrated here.[3] (Though sadly most of the texts I read aren't available in a format that allows me to use this tool.) All the strategies above help with my sequencing issues, but the other area that gives me particular trouble is my impaired working and visual memory. It's relatively easy to catch tracking and sequencing errors; they're superficial, mechanical glitches. Sometimes funny, sometimes annoying, but always relatively simple. Impaired working and visual memory is far trickier.

My first year of graduate school was a profound struggle as I grappled with challenging new material and drowned in the sheer volume of words and pages assigned for every class. To cope, I dropped a course and took incompletes in all but one of my classes.[4] More than anything else, my first encounter with literary theory shook my sense of self as a reader. It was as if I'd hit a wall. I'd spend three hours reading fewer than ten pages and still felt lost. For the first time since grade school, I was silent in class unless cold called. At the time, I worried I was simply too stupid for theory or perhaps my brain was just *wrong* for it somehow. But for a conversation with Maura Nolan, I would have

---

3   This effect doesn't translate well to a black-and-white page, alas.
4   For the first time since childhood, I was trying to get by unaccommodated since my diagnosis from high school was by then considered out of date. Testing would be hard to afford on a graduate stipend and my family was no longer in a financial position to help me. When it became clear that I wouldn't pass my qualifying exams without more time — and as a result I'd lose my fellowship — I took out a student loan to pay for my third diagnostic entirely out of pocket. Even on a sliding scale, it was $2,000.

left the program.[5] In retrospect, it was a problem not only of processing speed, but of visual and working memory. Most people can store quite a bit of information in their working memory, holding it suspended there while moving on; I cannot. For the most part, I either take the time to digest something fully — and then will remember it for an exceptionally long time — or I don't and it's gone very very quickly, especially if I consumed the information visually. Because theory was too dense and unfamiliar for me to digest quickly, between paragraph one and paragraph four of Saussure or Spivak it was as if I hadn't read the previous paragraphs at all. It was simply gone. And unlike a mechanical tracking error, this particular challenge was easy to interpret as mere intellectual inadequacy. Suddenly the strategies I'd long used on more familiar modes of writing weren't working. I had to develop new strategies and revisit old ones I'd long since abandoned. I went back to reading aloud to myself so I'd have two modes of sensory input: visual and auditory, especially helpful since my auditory processing and memory is far superior to the visual.[6] I also began taking extensive marginal notes. If the previous paragraph was going to disappear from my working

---

5 I was there to talk to Maura about fifteenth-century lyric poetry, but somehow the dam burst and I found myself telling her that I couldn't keep up with the course reading, that I have learning disabilities, that reading Derrida and Adorno was a hopeless experience, and that I might not be 'cut out for' a PhD. (I remember my eyes stinging and thinking the only thing that could make my outburst more embarrassing would be to actually *cry*.) Maura's gentle, unsentimental kindness was everything I needed — and she told me that I was a beautiful close reader. I clung to that phrase. I'm not a speed reader or a theoretical reader, but I'm a *close reader*.

6 Reading aloud, however, could be isolating, since I couldn't read aloud to myself in the library, a café, or in study meet-ups with my cohort.

memory, I'd have to process it, summarize it, and write that summary down, both so I could revisit it and so that I'd have a kinesthetic memory of the annotation. This practice is slow, but incredibly effective for me.[7] I became a passionate annotator.

Just imagine my delight when I discovered so many sixteenth-century readers, writers, and printers were equally passionate annotators! Both printed and scrawled in the margins of Reformation polemics, I found handy marginal glosses of the sort I'd write, both as the textual apparatus and as idiosyncratic additions that I learned paleography to transcribe. The more I learned about readers of the past the more variety I discovered, not only in individual readers, but as dominant reading practices have changed dramatically over time. Now reading silently is considered a marker of the transition from childish to mature reading, but before the development of spaces between words in the seventh century CE, it was entirely normative for Europeans to read aloud, sounding the letters out as they went.[8] I'd have fit right in! Perhaps if I'd read before the codex came to dominate, I could simply have unrolled a smaller portion of the scroll to reduce tracking errors, rather than covering up part of the page.

---

7   Here too economics play a role. As a grad student on a very limited stipend, I couldn't afford to buy an extensive library of expensive academic books and this presented quandaries. Could I ethically write (lightly in pencil) in library books? Or would that be damaging to someone else's reading? Could I afford to lose my annotations when I left Berkeley? Did I have the time and money for extensive photocopying — photocopying that would violate copyright? As an assistant professor at a well-endowed college, I now have the resources for a sizable library, but again my best adaptive strategies are painfully dependent on economic privilege.

8   Paul Saenger, *Space Between Words: The Origins of Silent Reading* (Stanford: Stanford University Press), 1–14.

And spelling was once so beautifully flexible! (I might have written "Theory filled me with 'despair,' 'despaire,' or 'despayre.'") I've come to feel incredibly connected to the readers of the past — like I'm a sixteenth-century reader plagued by scribal error — and I try to share this sense of connection to readers of the past with my students.

This is the first time I've shared these experiences and my strategies for reading with my colleagues. It has made me nervous enough I nearly withdrew the essay twice.[9] But I have been sharing all of this with my students since my first day as a TA. On the first day of class, when I remind students to give me any accommodation letters they may have, I tell them that I know the drill since I have a learning disability and was giving faculty my accommodation letter back in the Stone Age. I let them know that I may make transposition errors on the board or in handwritten comments: "So if my annotations on your paper don't quite make sense, try turning that 'b' into a 'd' or reversing a couple of letters, or of course, just ask. But don't worry! I have someone else double check my math before submitting final grades!" When I write on the board, I ask for help with spelling and invite students to catch my transcription errors. ("'Receive': r-e-c . . . ? Help! I don't know which vowel to buy now!" "Prof. Bahr? Don't you mean 3.1.45–90 not 1.3? It's in Act Three, isn't it?")[10] I've found that publicly asking for and accepting help from my students encourages them to accept help from me and their peers as well; trusting my students helps them trust me in return.

---

9 Writing this, I thought I could hear my high school teacher over my shoulder reciting: "Learning disabilities aren't real. It's a bogus diagnosis purchased by wealthy parents . . ."

10 My spelling is always poor, but exponentially so when writing on the board since I can't rely on the kinesthetic, muscle memory of having written it correctly so many times in the past. Only on the board would I now misspell 'thanks' or 'with.'

Most neurotypical (or undiagnosed) students have never recieved the detailed study of how their brains work that I have, so I encourage them to try different things and discover what works for them, and whether they're naturally inclined to visual, auditory, or kinesthetic learning.[11] I encourage them to try some of the strategies I use, like reading aloud, annotating heavily, or using Beeline Reader. Some students have found my techniques unexpectedly helpful, while others have not; either way, I hope that engaging my strategies will help students adopt an experimental mindset and thus discover something on their own. (A student with anxiety recently told me that she wore an eye mask to start writing her paper so that she couldn't see the daunting blank page or second guess every word that she typed as she saw it appear on the screen.)

TL;DR — Ultimately, I want my students (and colleagues) to know that it's ok to admit that reading is hard and that there is no one way to read. Sometimes I need to be reminded of this too.[12]

---

11 I try to keep these three modalities in mind while teaching too. For example, when teaching essay structure, I practice repetition with variation: first I give a lecture and ask students to take their own notes; I then give a formal handout with the same basic content; and last, when I email them about preparations for next class, I briefly recap the lecture with more informal diction. This sequence accommodates strongly auditory, kinesthetic, and visual learners, while giving all students three separate formulations to help them assimilate difficult material.

12 I'd like to extend my thanks to Kaitlin Heller and Suzanne Akbari for bringing this volume together and Chris Piuma for his hard work on the difficult layout for this piece. I'd also like to thank Maura Nolan once more for ensuring I stayed in grad school and David Landreth whose unflagging support and advocacy ensured that I finished it. And my family, always and forever. Let's get together for some Twiggins.

Alexandra Atiya

Text to Speech

When I first graduated from college in 2007, I started working for a writer who is blind. I was a part-time weekend reader, which meant that I would show up on Saturday or Sunday mornings and read the newspaper, starting with the front-page headlines and the business section, the *New York Review of Books*, the *Nation*, and a weekly investment rag called *Barron's*. I would also read anything else that needed to be read: mail, instruction manuals, invoices, opera librettos, notes. Sometimes I read books, though less often then you might think on account of the availability of commercial audio books and the Library of Congress Talking Books service, which mails recorded books to Americans who have vision loss or other disabilities that make using print books difficult.

He generally employed a human reader when a text was so difficult that it required recourse to footnotes or other supplements or was too new or obscure to have been recorded.

Initially I thought I'd do the job for a few months, at most, but I ended up working for him for seven years until I moved to Toronto for graduate school. At points I worked full-time but mostly I worked part-time, often with big gaps. In that seven-year period, I also volunteered as a reader at The Lighthouse, an organization that provides health services and other assistance to blind or visually impaired New Yorkers.

These experiences changed the way I read. They also happened in a period in which reading technologies, even mass-market ones, changed considerably. Going mostly on instinct, without thinking too much about it, I ended up experimenting with new ways of reading that have stayed with me even after I have returned to being a student.

The longer I worked for the writer, the more types of things I read. He tended to read the tougher things during the week. As a result, when I started working more hours I began to read more literature, which had to be read in different way than the speedy way I read newspapers and magazines.

The first serious thing I remember reading aloud was *Moby-Dick*, which I read with a special dictionary of nautical terms. I had attempted the novel before but never gotten very far. Now I was starting toward the end of the book and stopping every few minutes to repeat a sentence or look up a word. I probably only got through 15 or 20 pages but the story was so vivid that I found it completely enveloping. The ineffability of these reading experiences makes them frustrating to write about. I had the feeling of being inside the story, on the ship, if that makes any sense. I also remember reading *Henry IV* and *King Lear* and other Shakespeare plays, including every word of every footnote. It was a demanding, inscriptive way of reading. I discovered, in this process, that some writers I thought I didn't like (Faulkner) or couldn't quite understand (Joyce) came magnificently alive in reading aloud.

That said, the reading process was mostly mechanical. I never felt that I was narrating anything — I never did voices or attempted to put any emotion into what I read. I tried to read as quickly and neutrally as possible. I read certain types of punctuation, but only the marks that were necessary to understand the meaning of a sentence. Periods and commas could be marked by a brief pause. Semicolons and hyphens basically disappeared. But I had to read colons, dashes, exclamation points, quotation marks, sometimes even question marks. One example — if I had to read the following sentence (which comes from a recent *New York Times* article that I chose simply because it happened to contain a variety of punctuation marks):

> His autobiography, "Clock This: My Life as an Inventor," was published in 1999.
>
> In 2000, Mr. Baylis walked 100 miles across the Namib Desert — partly for a charitable cause, but also to demonstrate a new invention, electric shoes.[1]

I would read it as:

> his autobiography quote clock this colon my life as an inventor end quote was published in nineteen ninety nine in two thousand mister baylis walked a hundred miles across the namib

---

[1] Neil Genzlinger. "Trevor Baylis, Inventor of a Radio Powered by Muscle, Dies at 80," *The New York Times*, March 7, 2018, https://www.nytimes.com/2018/03/07/obituaries/trevor-baylis-inventor-of-a-radio-powered-by-muscle-dies-at-80.html

> desert dash partly for a charitable cause but also
> to demonstrate a new invention electric shoes

I had the feeling of being a technical tool in a process. I keep using the first-person singular to describe it here, but at the time it didn't feel like that. It was someone else reading, but I was the voice. When I first interviewed at The Lighthouse, the volunteer coordinator gave me a cheerful warning: You're not going to be reading the next Patricia Cornwell! People come in and think that's what this is, and they end up very disappointed! I knew what she meant. *You don't get to choose. It's not about you.*

Much as I believed at the time that I could make it *not about me*, I now find myself writing about how my experience transformed the way I read. I don't claim to understand the experiences of readers with vision loss, and I don't aim in this essay to tell their stories; only they can. But there is something in my own experience that I want to share, in part because I found myself exploring something I was deeply curious about, a type of reading antithetical to any I had previously undertaken. It was far apart from the typical poles of reading for pleasure and reading for work. Reading for pleasure is often described as escapism, as forgetting yourself. The implication is that you'll never be held to account for what you've read. On the other hand, reading in preparation for work (academia, law, drama, business, politics, etc.) requires that we think, on some level, about our public or professional image while we read, and the necessity of self-preservation makes us read more intensely in order to avoid the public embarrassment of misreading a text or demonstrating only a very shallow understanding of it.

In these circumstances, I felt liberated from analyzing or judging what I read. At the same time, the mechanics of reading aloud forced me to pay complete attention — nothing could be truly skimmed — and engage deeply with the language. In a sense, reading aloud was almost like translating or reading in a foreign language, when a lot of effort is expended just to get the right words out there, when you have to ruminate just to get to the end of a sentence. Questions of anything other than the most superficial meaning get pushed to the side, to be answered at some later time. I remember once the writer had me read some Chekhov stories whose mood was intriguing but whose meaning completely eluded me. After each one he would ask me (uncharacteristically) what I thought the story meant and I had no answer, and we would just continue without answering.

In this same seven-year period, I acquired my first Kindle: one of the early versions, which was not like a tablet. It wasn't backlit and it didn't feel like a screen. It was mostly usable for reading Amazon-compatible e-books or rich text files, although it did have a short list of "experimental" functions. One of these functions was a text-to-speech reader, which would read any book aloud in a robotic voice.

I *loved* it. I listened to it while I read visually. It mispronounced things, it messed up words, the pacing was weird, but I couldn't get enough of it. I had never liked audiobooks because they were too slow and dramatic and because I preferred audio as a supplement to visual reading rather than as a replacement. But in those early Kindles I found my ideal. When it got to the end of a page, it would flash to the next one and continue reading, which meant that it was effectively a page turning technology as well. I could do tedious tasks, like washing dishes or chopping vegetables, while listening to it and reading the pages. And when I wasn't occupied, it paced me and made me slow down.

I felt for a little while that I had found an almost utopian way of reading: simultaneously visual and auditory and completely un-interpretative. This was not solely because of the computerized voice and its implication of impartiality. I felt I had been granted access to books without all the insinuations about the status of author and the temperament of the reader implied by covers, blurbs, bindings, layout, and font. The Kindle used the same font, applied the same flat voice to everything. You could adjust font size and voice speed (and, I later found out, gender of the automated voice) but it was much more uniform than printed books. I felt that I had finally uncovered a pure form of a book, comprised of only voice and text, stripped of affect and design.

Most people I knew were sort of appalled at my love for the Kindle. Don't you know what damage it does to the publishing industry? The name alone is horrifying — one friend told me — isn't it telling you to burn your books? My roommate, a painter, was maybe more baffled than appalled: he read a lot and loved the physical qualities of books, and he couldn't understand how I got any warmth out of that thing. He nevertheless gave me a small painting of myself with the Kindle in hand (the frontispiece of this essay).

Like all utopias, though, it was short lived. I was on a rush-hour bus into New Jersey when it died on me out of the blue and I never quite forgave it for abandoning me in the middle of an excruciatingly slow trip. The newer basic Kindles don't have the text-to-speech function anymore, although the tablet-like Kindles apparently do. I'm not sure whether Amazon eliminated the text-to-speech function because most people didn't like it or because of pushback from organizations like the Authors Guild, who argued that it infringed upon the sales of professional audiobooks. I still kept using a Kindle, but never as zealously as I had at first.

It was interesting to see, in that period, how new technologies affected the reading habits of people I knew. Some friends stopped reading. Smartphones were arriving, the markets were crashing, it was hard to focus. They only ever seemed to read a book if there was a Wi-Fi outage, and then they read intensely. Curiously those friends were the most adamant that listening to a book, being read to, was not the same thing as reading. Others, particularly those whose jobs involved physical work, were finding more sources of potential audiobooks. One friend, a visual artist, used to bike all over the city while listening to the Kindle, and then in the studio he would listen to a crowd-sourced audiobook site, where groups of amateur readers would each contribute a chapter of a popular text (the one I remember most was *Frankenstein*). In a way, it made me feel that even though we had been learning about reading since kindergarten, none of us really knew what it was anymore nor how it would figure into our later lives.

It was indisputable that most people I knew were reading less, and yet at the same time, it was clear that digitization — the thing usually identified as the destroyer of reading habits — was also making reading more accessible. Screen readers like JAWS had been, for decades, offering the possibility of reading a wider variety of material and correspondence, and the proliferation of personal devices and assistive technologies allowed access to massive libraries with greater ease and accuracy.

The combination of reading aloud and using the Kindle seemed to open up my mind to books I had previously resisted. I had been a secretive reader, one who rarely took recommendations (or quietly resented it if I did). In this seven-year period I started to read all kinds of things I thought I couldn't read because I had previously thought they were too slow and too, for lack of a better word, obvious. Now I could get to the far reaches of Thomas Hardy, George Eliot, Anthony Trollope. I sometimes recorded what I read, not because I wanted anyone else to listen to it, but because reading aloud had become one of my ways of reading.

—§—

I recently found a short video I made during this period. I was cooking in my kitchen in New York and I had dropped an egg. The Kindle kept reading to me. Evidently something about this moment struck me because I recorded it, albeit in a terrible, grainy video. It's an exceptionally bright, sunny day. My legs are visible only as a shadow stretching across the broken, yolky egg on my green linoleum floor and I turn toward the Kindle, which is flatly voicing *Washington Square* and adding pauses at strange moments:

> well what do you advise me now to be very
> patient to watch and wait and is that bad advice
> or good that is not for me to say mrs penniman
> rejoined with some dignity...

Next to the Kindle are appliances and comfort objects that got lost in my move to Toronto: the tray my grandparents brought back from Egypt, the little metal stallion that my roommate had brought back from Pakistan and which we used to hold our kitchen towel in place. Watching the video — hearing that now-lost voice that had accompanied me for several years — conjured up an overwhelming memory of the room and time, a sense of the irretrievability of how I used to read.

— § —

Reading for graduate school was a big adjustment. Even before I started classes, I realized that my way of reading had changed from when I was an undergrad. When I was prepping for the Literature GRE subject test, I had to read short samples of canonical works and identify them. Some I could identify by the character names, scenario or style, but the only ones I identified immediately, without even thinking about it, were the ones I had read aloud in a repetitious way. It's hard to describe how it felt to recognize those passages. The sensation that comes to mind is the reverberation of a bell.

It was hard for me to come back to reading for academic purposes, because to some extent I had become accustomed to close reading everything. But for some things it has proved useful. Whenever I need to analyze a passage in detail, I force myself to take the time and read it aloud multiple times. It has made me space out my reading — I think it has given me a sense of how much time it takes to read, and how reading quickly is not universally valuable.

In a sense, it created a second register of reading that was at once both rigorous and very free. At a party last year, I somehow ended up telling an English PhD student about how I'd read those sections of *Moby-Dick*. She told me that reading so that you understood every superficial reference was called *surface reading*, and I was irrationally pleased that there was a name for what I'd done, that it could be seen as one mode of reading among many.

And it expanded my concept of reading as an act confined to a book. It made me consider why I thought a pure form of book existed, and why I thought that pure form involved a text stripped of anything but its words. Why I thought that the truest form of reading was somehow anti-visual, when at the same time, I was recognizing its inherent visuality by volunteering to be the visual interface for others.

I no longer have an automated reader, but I still sometimes find myself searching for crowdsourced online recordings to listen to as I read visually. Hearing voices from all over the world reading to one another feels nothing like hearing a single, automated voice, but it retains some of the raw, amateurish feeling that drew me in, the captivating sense that reading is not static, controlled, and disappearing, but changeable and communal, able to be expanded and reinvented as we go along.

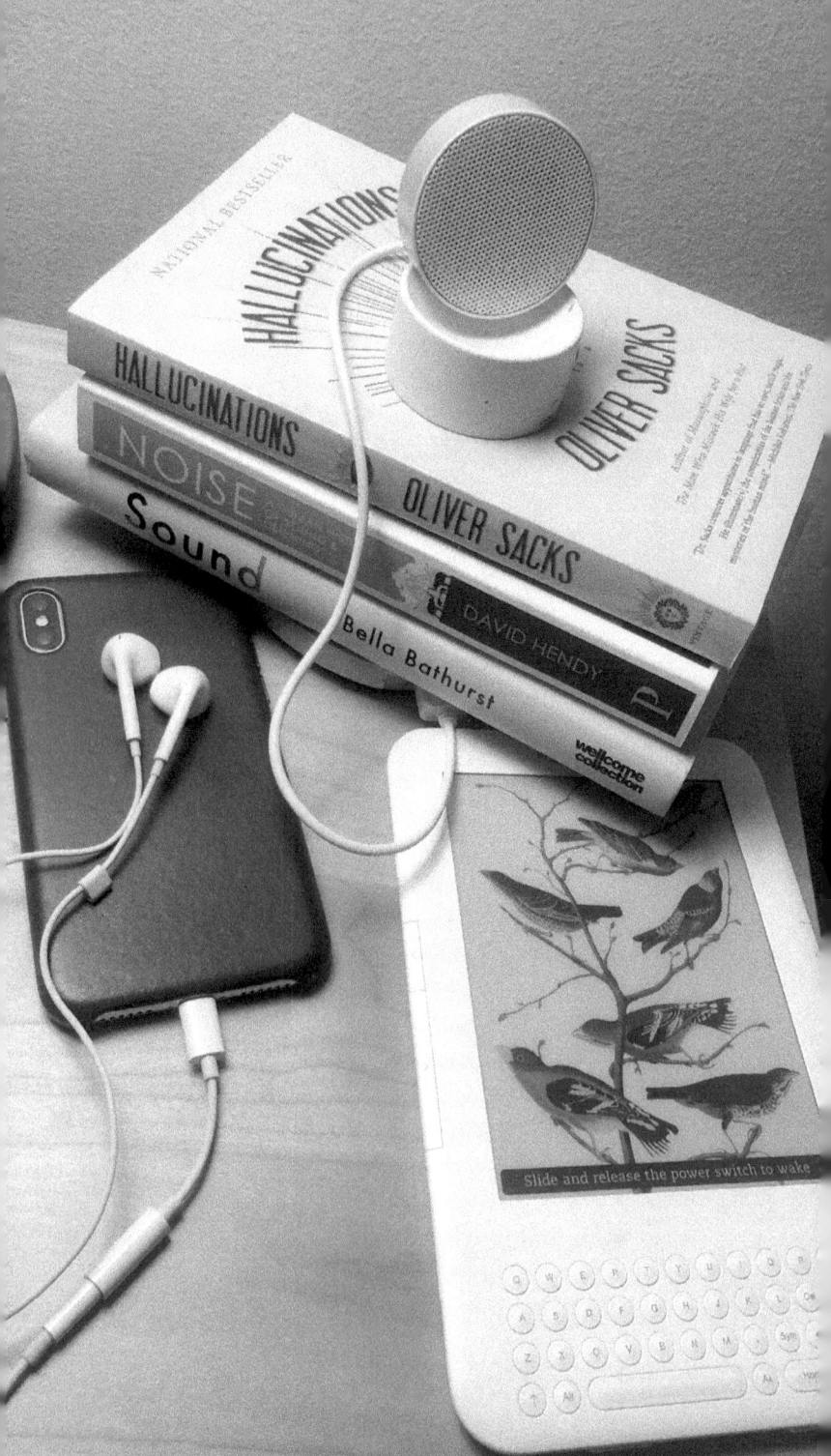

Jonathan Hsy

Phantom Sounds

A few years ago (in early March 2017, to be exact), my relationship to sound — and reading — began to change. I woke up one day to a constant high-pitched ringtone that I initially mistook for a distant alarm, but I soon realized there was nothing actually "making" the sound I was hearing. This kind of experience of phantom sound is commonly known as tinnitus (from the Latin verb *tinnere* "to ring"), usually defined in technical terms as a sensation of noise without an external stimulus. The initial ringtone sound eventually went away, but tinnitus has been my odd companion ever since, coming and going erratically depending on physical and environmental conditions (seasonal, architectural, acoustic). Sometimes tinnitus feels like the roaring of waves or hum of machinery; sometimes it's a screechy wheel or chirping crickets. Whatever form it takes, tinnitus can be especially intrusive in externally quiet environments (bedroom, office, library) — making it difficult for me to concentrate and read.

IMAGE: My bedside table, March 2019. A little sound machine makes ambient white noise. It rests on top of a few paperback books next to my mobile device (for audiobooks and podcasts) and an e-reader (mostly for novels, poetry, and nonfiction). PHOTO: Jonathan Hsy.

When tinnitus first emerged in life, my first impulse was to *do a bunch of research and read a lot about it* (yes, I'm an academic). Truth be told, much of this entailed scouring online forums and discovering it's not an unusual thing for people to experience at some point or another — and I was surprised to discover from some Deaf friends via social media and in-person conversations that it's not unusual for them to experience tinnitus as well (this fact nicely challenges preconceived notions that "deafness" simply means complete silence).[1] As the bothersome tinnitus persisted and I consulted different physicians and specialists, I learned how health professionals approach this phenomenon: as a somatic condition, an embodied experience, or even a "phantom disability."[2] In addition to seeking medical care (if a "cause" can be discerned: nerve damage? illness? allergies? stress?), people who experience tinnitus can also aim to manage their surroundings to adapt to the condition or engage in cognitive behavioral therapy — that is, find strategies to change how they *think about* and *react to* the unsettling reality of phantom sounds.[3]

My own main strategy for coping with distracting "extra sound" is — ironically enough — to fill my personal space with *more* sound. The little sound machine that I

---

1 Louise Wheeler and Andrew Glyn Hopwood, "Tinnitus: A Deafhearing Phenomenon," *Qualitative Inquiry* 21.2 (2015): 173–74.
2 David Baguley et al., *Tinnitus: A Multidisciplinary Approach*, 2nd ed. (Chichester, UK: Wiley-Blackwell, 2013); Mack Hogood, "Disability and Biotranslation: Tinnitus as Phantom Disability," in *Disability Media Studies*, ed. Elizabeth Ellcessor and Bill Kirkpatrick (New York University Press, 2017), 311–29.
3 Mack Hagood, "Listening to Tinnitus: Roles of Media When Hearing Breaks Down," *Sounding Out!* July 16, 2012, https://soundstudiesblog.com/2012/07/16/listening-to-tinnitus-roles-of-media-when-hearing-breaks-down/

keep on my bedside table, along with whatever happens to be my leisure reading at the moment, produces just the right amount of white noise (something like the hum of a fan) to mask the "internal" sounds that I hear. I also take this device with me from home into the office or wherever I might be working, as I can never quite predict when I might need the gadget to help me concentrate.

My experiments sonically altering my environment have taught me that reading aurally (i.e., listening to audiobooks and podcasts) can be an important form of self-care. When I listen to audiobooks — usually when I'm winding down at night, or if I'm passing the time in transit — I can feel a welcome relief in "escaping" into a narrative and thus distracting myself from the annoyance of tinnitus. I can take pleasure in *relaxing* and being surrounded by another's voice. Over time, I've realized that reading aurally hones my skills in "close listening" too — I attend more carefully to the crafted quality of texts and appreciate how the people voicing texts aloud are performing for an audience.[4]

Perhaps what I'm describing is not so much the practical benefits of sonic "distraction" but rather the beguiling intimacies of aural reading, or "being read to," or something that might be called "reading-listening." In her beautiful, thoughtful contribution, Alexandra reflects on her experience reading texts aloud for readers who are blind or visually impaired, and she describes forgetting herself (putting aside her ego) as she focused on mediating the textual voices of others.[5] As a hearing and sighted reader increasingly choosing to listen to texts, how might I reflect on what forgetting myself means as a reader-listener?

---

4   Jonathan Hsy, "Close Listening: Talking Books, Blind Readers, and Medieval Worldbuilding," *postmedieval* 7.2 (2016): 181–92.

5   See page 86 of this volume.

Over the years I've tried using screen-readers and similar technologies that convert digital text into synthesized speech, but I just haven't been able to train myself to adapt to such modes. I know various people — blind and sighted — who prefer *or require* such technologies to read texts effectively, and some can read very quickly in doing so; access needs vary from person to person and should be respected. For my part — and I can only speak for myself — I appreciate the "human touch" I can access by reading a voiced text aurally.

One of my favorite books about the intimacies of listening-reading is by the professor and memoirist Georgina Kleege. *Sight Unseen* (1999), Kleege's first-person reflections on her own blindness, is a classic in contemporary disability studies. In a discussion of books on tape (in the days before digital audiobooks or online podcasts), Kleege notes how vocally produced recordings of books "perhaps satisfy an impossible longing... you can have storytime any time, wherever you please" and listening to a book on portable headphones means you "can wrap yourself in a cocoon of comforting narrative, which provides continuity to your disjointed day."[6] Reading aloud not only creates a transformative dwelling space ("cocoon") but is also what Kleege calls a "theatrical performance" of a voice with an audience: even the "most neutral, unpolished reading adds a third dimension to the encounter between reader and text."[7]

When I read Alexandra's reflections, I was struck by the efforts she made to keep her voice as neutral as possible and not to "upstage" the text being vocalized. As a

---

6 Georgina Kleege, *Sight Unseen* (New Haven: Yale University Press, 1999), 171.
7 Kleege, *Sight Unseen*, 172.

listener-reader, I don't mind the humanity of the vocal mediator coming through; in fact, I often feel *more* engaged with a text when I'm invited to think self-consciously about "listening through" the recorded sonic voice to the textual written voice being conveyed. The experience of aurally reading a vocally mediated text reminds me of the somewhat asynchronous "real time" experience of watching a live interpreter (speaking or signing) embody the voice or narration of another person. I can't *not* pay attention to what the mediator is doing just as I attend to the voice being conveyed. For me, reading aurally is not so much a two-way relationship between a text and audience as much as it is a dynamic choreography of text, vocal reader, and aural reader.

The constellation of issues I consider here — reading, community, intimacy, and access — are shaped by my professional background in the academic field of disability studies and also by my commitments to disability activism. Mia Mingus, a disability justice organizer who identifies as queer and physically disabled, has given the name "access intimacy" to "that elusive, hard to describe feeling when someone else 'gets' your access needs," and it "can happen with complete strangers, disabled or not, or sometimes it can be built over years."[8] The time, care, and labor that professional and volunteer voice readers perform in addressing the access needs of strangers or audiences they have never even met suggests access intimacy on a broad scale — and this all of serves as a reminder that access intimacy need not entail physical proximity.

---

8 Mia Mingus, "Access Intimacy: The Missing Link." *Leaving Evidence*, May 5, 2011, https://leavingevidence.wordpress.com/2011/05/05/access-intimacy-the-missing-link/

The recent nonprofessional audiobook of *Resistance and Hope: Essays by Disabled People* (2018) edited by Alice Wong on behalf of the Disability Visibility Project is an especially vivid example of access intimacy by and for a diverse disability community.[9] This collection — available as an ebook, PDF, and audiobook — features essays by disabled writers, artists, and activists, with the audiobook format physically recording and combining disabled voices. The book's mode of production aptly pursues disability justice: all royalties from purchases of the book will support HEARD (Helping to Advance the Rights of Deaf Communities), an organization that seeks to correct and prevent wrongful convictions of individuals who are d/Deaf or hard of hearing. This effort to uphold the rights of disabled people — including the rights of incarcerated d/Deaf people to have full access to sign language interpreters or appropriate means of communication — cultivates an ethos of access intimacy. One rewarding experience for me as I listen to the *Resistance and Hope* audiobook is hearing the physical voices of disabled activists such as Alice Wong whom I have never met in person but nonetheless feel I "know" through Twitter and social media.

Regardless of whether (or whither) it goes, tinnitus — or rather, my wavering and wobbly experience of it — is perpetually shifting how I read (and think) about sound, orality, and aurality. The fifteenth-century *Book of Margery Kempe*, an English housewife's dictated spiritual autobiography (and a work to which I repeatedly return in my teaching and research), makes a curious distinction between the idea of "bodily" [physical] voices and "gostly"

---

9 Alice Wong, ed., *Resistance and Hope: Essays By Disabled People* (N.p.: Disability Visibility Project, 2018). https://disabilityvisibilityproject.com/resist/

IMAGE: Margery Kempe's beloved St. Margaret's church in King's Lynn, July 2015. I remember the fragrance of its wooden beams and furnishings, and the ambient sounds reverberating throughout the space.
PHOTO: Jonathan Hsy.

[spiritual] voices; such a demarcation evokes the writings of mystic Richard Rolle, whose books were read aloud to Kempe by her scribe.[10] There's an extensive history of scholarship on Margery Kempe that seeks to "diagnose" her experience of hearing voices and "gostly" sounds (epilepsy? psychosis? hallucinations?).[11] What fascinates me about this text is not any prospect of "diagnosis," nor even Kempe's parsing of "objective" and "subjective" sound (eerily like

---

10 Lynn Staley, ed., *The Book of Margery Kempe* (Kalamazoo, MI: Medieval Institute Publications, 1996), I.58, 3391–92. https://d.lib.rochester.edu/teams/text/staley-book-of-margery-kempe-book-i-part-ii. Rolle makes a distinction between "gostly" song experienced inwardly vs. "vtward songe" that is "formyd with bodily eris to be hard" [heard]. Richard Rolle, *The Fire of Love* [*De Incendio Amoris*], ed. Ralph Harvey (London: Kegan Paul, Trench, Trübner & Co., 1896), II.3.19 (p. 73).
11 Corinne Saunders and Charles Fernyhough, "Reading Margery Kempe's Inner Voices," *postmedieval* 8.2 (2017): 209–17.

IMAGE: Shadowy formations of the Grand Canyon after sunrise, October 2017. I remember the cold morning air, the slowly shifting light across the landscape, and the constant hum of tinnitus.
PHOTO: Jonathan Hsy.

tinnitus?), but the idea that Kempe had internalized her discursive frameworks for sound aurally.

The Book of Margery Kempe is mediated through, and by, recursive modalities of reading experience. Throughout the *Book*'s production, Kempe dictated her own reflections and had her own newly mediated words read back to her: a familiar yet alien version of her own voice embodied by another person. In reflecting on my experience of tinnitus and historical reading experience, might I be moving toward some medieval expression of access intimacy?

I am now comfortable saying that tinnitus is something I live with, whether or not it's present with me at all times. It might go away in the future, or it may morph into something else — but I'm always-already prepared for its re-arrival.

As I re-read *The Book of Margery Kempe* with complexities of sound in mind, I have come to appreciate the dynamic recursivity of oral and aural dimensions of reading across time and space. How we read (i.e., the physical mechanics and technologies of reading) operates in a "feedback loop" with how we read (how we absorb and interpret texts). I value tremendously the intimacies of reading and thinking with others.

Brown
The Rise of Western Chr
TENTH ANNIVERSARY REVISE
FRANZEN
POEMS OF ARAB ANDALUS
Bartlett
Why Can the Dead Do Such Great Things?
Cameron
the Byzantines

Kirsty Schut

On Not Being a Voracious Reader

Content note: trichotillomania.

My long-term roommate is a voracious reader, of the sort I was as a child and thought I always would be. The sort of person who has a book to read on the bus and a second one in her purse in case she gets through it too quickly, plus a few on the Kindle for backup. She uses the public library's hold system as a private reading list in a way that isn't quite what the original designers intended, but no one's called her out on it yet. She has a knack for leaving the right books on the kitchen table when I'm having a hard time or just because she thinks I'll like them. She makes my world bigger, and I am grateful. It's an act of love that I don't think I repay very well with the academic tomes I sometimes leave there for breakfast reading. I got through André Vauchez's *Sainthood in the Later Middle Ages* that way one semester, a few pages at a time, and a good chunk of Charles Taylor's *A Secular Age*.[1] She did

---

1   André Vauchez, *Sainthood in the Later Middle Ages*, trans. Jane Birrell (Cambridge: Cambridge University Press, 1997); Charles Taylor, *A Secular Age* (Cambridge, Mass.: Bellknap Press of Harvard University Press, 2007).

IMAGE: Breakfast at the author's end of the table.
PHOTO: Kirsty Schut.

gleefully Instagram a pile of books from my saints phase a little while ago (the shiny gold cover of Robert Bartlett's *Why Can The Dead Do Such Great Things?* next to Laura Ackerman Smoller's award-winning — and illustrated — *The Saint and the Chopped-Up Baby*) so I know that she's getting *something* out of it sometimes.[2] But piling up books and reading them are different things, and I feel I do much more of the former than the latter these days.

I grew up a bookish child in a bookish family. I don't know whether I actually remember learning to read or whether it's one of those memories that builds itself up out of stories you've been told. It was September, cold enough for one sweater, just starting to get dark outside. There was a burr bush at the base of the old apple tree in the backyard, and it looked so fluffy and pillowy that I just had to fling myself backwards into it, and I do remember that mid-air feeling of "maybe I shouldn't be doing this," but by then of course it was too late. When I was extracted, with some tears and panic, my hair was a tangleful of burrs. My mother took me inside and sat me down on the floor with a pile of books (my favourite toy) to play with. She removed the burrs and I figured out phonics. I was three and a half years old.

Reading was prohibited at the dinner table or while crossing the road; anywhere else was fair game. One brother tried taping paperbacks to the outside of the shower; I experimented with hanging up laundry with *Harry Potter* in one hand. When my youngest brother was

---

[2] Robert Bartlett, *Why Can The Dead Do Such Great Things? Saints and Worshippers from the Martyrs to the Reformation* (Princeton: Princeton University Press, 2013); Laura Ackerman Smoller, *The Saint and the Chopped-Up Baby: The Cult of Vincent Ferrer in Medieval and Early Modern Europe* (Ithaca: Cornell University Press, 2014).

dragging his heels on reading one summer, our mother set up a sticker reward system in which everyone in the house got a treat for every ten books that he read aloud. His three elder siblings chased him around the house with piles of picture books: "Thomas, we want a chocolate!" The family legend of the great-great-grandmother who gave herself pneumonia by staying up late in the week before Christmas trying to read all the books she was giving to people never seemed terribly implausible. Reading was something we did, like breathing. It was who I was, and who we were.

The voracious reading slowed for me — never stopped, but slowed to a trickle — when I started a creative writing program at an arts high school in eleventh grade. There wasn't *time*, for one thing. I was commuting with my father over an hour each way, and I get carsick; most often I'd just sleep. There was the homework and studying, a bit of a shock to the system after two years of homeschooling and no tests. There was the perpetual sleep deprivation as I learned how to write poetry under the pressure of a deadline, and how to pull my first all-nighters. But it was also something of a conscious choice. In my daily writing, I found myself taking on the voices of the authors I was reading too easily, the same way that I was imprinting on accents I heard in movies at the time. With one-off writing practices it wasn't a problem; our training came in part from emulating specific elements of things that we read as a group. But in longer pieces, things that needed weeks or months to create, I couldn't keep the style of the writing stable. I needed to draw back and find my own writer's voice. There was a sense of loss as I did that, but also a sense of excitement and discovery. I had to admit that it worked.

It is one of the few regrets of my life that in a ruthless bout of post–high school tidying up, I went through my Literary Arts binders and threw away everything that we'd read in those two years. At the time, I was sure I'd remember the names of things I'd want to come back to later, and that's what the internet is for, right? There was also some existential purging going on. High school was good for me in many ways — I'd made friends for the first time since I was six, for one thing — but it had also stressed me out to the point that I'd pulled out all my eyebrows. The friends, bless 'em, didn't care. But anything that renders you shuddering with tears over the bathroom sink, struggling to summon the breath to repeat "you are a good and beautiful person who is worthy of love" to your swollen face in the mirror, is bound to leave behind a few demons to exorcise.

It's hard to be articulate about something that doesn't respond to reason. I don't want to make a metaphor out of it, about reading and self-destruction or reading and loss of self, about idle hands and the devil's work, about making one's mark on the page. If I read for any length of time, there'll be a pile of hair on the floor. That's all. Trichotillomania has always been tied to my reading practice to some degree. Sometimes this has been a source of great distress and sometimes — most of the time, the past few years — it has simply been a fact of life. Keep a garbage can to the left of you while reading or writing. Wash your face with cold water when the pressure behind your eyelashes gets too intense. Generalized tugging is better than searching for targets. The best I can do to describe it is this: *Feels wrong. Fix. Repeat.* The last is the most important part. One day in grad school I came across a book in the university library that bore the unmistakeable traces of someone else doing the same thing. Shaking with shame and recognition, I put it back on the shelf. I still haven't read it.

If high school was bad for reading, university was worse. When I was truly reading all the time for school, as it seemed in undergrad, it was the last thing I wanted to do for fun. I say that, and yet... I remember saying rapturously to my father on the commute home in first or second year that all you really need for a university is a big library and some places for discussion. There were the required readings in undergrad: kneeling in front of the kitchen fireplace past midnight in first year, one chocolate chip per chapter of the Bible; standing over an art history textbook perched on the corner of the table in second; in an English bed with *Don Juan* in third; in my grandmother's empty house with Gitta Sereny's *Into that Darkness* in fourth year, in the midst of a snowstorm, while the grandmother in question descended further into dementia at home.[3] Course reserves photocopied and skimmed before an 8:30 class, my early morning buddy with his breakfast burrito doing the same thing across the table. Dante season in second year, the spring that I turned eighteen: *Inferno* in the passport office; *Purgatory* in the library with the Doré illustrations spread out before me and Sayers' translation in my lap; the ending of *Paradise* under the grubby skylight beneath the library on a hectic morning in March.

And then there were the non-required readings. Being a commuter student meant that I had a lot of time to kill on campus and, too shy to cross the threshold of the common room until fourth year, I killed that time dead in the library. I wouldn't even make it to a desk sometimes, slipping one

---

[3] Gitta Sereny, *Into That Darkness: An Examination of Conscience* (New York: Vintage Books, 1983).

item after another off the shelf and devouring them right there in the stacks, greedy, luxuriating in the freedom of choice. The first few years were spent catching up on all the poets I'd discovered in passing in high school. Michael Ondaatje, Leonard Cohen, Michael Crummey—I guess that one CanLit class did stick with me. My best friend was doing a theatre degree in Toronto; I went down to visit her in November of first year, saw a play by Daniel MacIvor, and spent the next few years browsing the Canadian theatre section whenever I had time, eventually branching out into Europe. I was very nearly late for a Hindu Aesthetics class because I was lingering over something by Christopher Fry. I was so mad at the prof who lent me his copy of *The Nine Tailors* when he learned I'd done bell ringing on my year abroad.[4] I was secretly grateful for the sanction to screw up my sleep schedule over something with a plot, but didn't he know that late October was no time to be giving a fourth-year student extra pages to read? Summers were for novels, a few, sometimes painfully. School-time was for poetry, plays, short stories, snatched in the times when I was surrounded by books, too tired for schoolwork, but unable to think of anything to do but read.

I've been a student for over two decades now. The rhythms of the school year have shaped nearly all of my life, and even when I lose my student status (*deo volente*) I suspect it will take some time for September to lose the sense of new beginnings, and early summer the sense of release from captivity. As a child, the end of the school year was marked by cupcakes and a trip to the library. I carefully planned out my first book of summer each year in high school and undergrad. I remember some of those

---

4   Dorothy L. Sayers, *The Nine Tailors* (London: Gollancz, 1934).

books distinctly, and the feeling that went with them: a bit self-conscious and awkward settling into it, like the first walk without a jacket, or the first swim in the lake. Tongue-in-cheek summer reading lists from professors (E.M. Forster's *A Room With a View*, recommended as a follow-up to the *Divine Comedy* with the tagline "On finding happiness in Florence"). Gifts that had piled up over the school year (Thomas King's *Medicine River*, handed down from a friend's English course on "The Canadian Small Town"). Guilt trips that had spanned the better half of a decade (A.S. Byatt's *Possession*, recommended by a teacher at my high school *audition*: the first thing I read after undergrad, which simultaneously made me weep for the creative parts of myself that I'd forgotten and confirmed that I was doing exactly the right thing in going to graduate school).[5]

Grad school, and the later years of the PhD especially, comes with a certain amount of unmooring from that temporal structure, not to mention a few other things. The post-grading palate cleanser fulfills something of the same function as the first book of summer, perhaps, but to a large extent the distinctions between term times and holidays are blurred. After all, you can always be writing your thesis; can always be reading another article, another book, another shamefully neglected classic in your field. Even the awestruck, hungry library browsing has had to be curtailed. I remember the feeling of heartbreak when a venerable committee member told me that the directive he'd given me as a master's student to "waste time in the library" was

---

5 E.M. Forster, *A Room With a View* (London: Edward Arnold, 1908); Thomas King, *Medicine River* (Markham: Viking Canada, 1989); A.S. Byatt, *Possession: A Romance* (London: Chatto & Windus, 1990).

over, and now it was time for "seek and destroy missions only." Pleasure reading, these last few years, has come to feel like an act of defiance against the voice in the head that chants "you ought, you ought."

I say that I'm not a voracious reader, and yet the whole breakfast book thing started because if I *don't* have something to turn the pages of for the four minutes it takes me to eat my toast, I *will* pick up *The Joy of Cooking* and start reading it, which is often entertaining (clambake for twenty on the beach?!), but occasionally nauseating for a life-long vegetarian. That's a grad school development. Maybe it's because I'm reading less and writing more, so there's room to want it again. Maybe it's because the act of reading calms the urge to be doing something useful, and my morning brain will accept instruction on the dangers and delights of rosin-boiled potatoes as a substitute for something work-related.

Breakfast books aside, my work reading tends to be deliberate and active. It needs both hands free, and a couple of pieces of equipment, for note-taking, or book-marking endnotes, or looking things up in passing. It's best done in the library, occasionally at home on the couch or at the table, but never in bed, and best not on the computer if I want to focus or remember. I pay more attention if I'm leaning forward in my chair — a technique I learned for test-taking in early undergrad, but it works here too, much to the detriment of my back. No matter how much I'm enjoying myself, which I genuinely am quite often, I've always got an eye on the page numbers, counting down to the end.

Grad school pleasure reading, on the other hand, comes with less ceremony and more serendipity. I lose an afternoon to an unplanned novel now and then, like the piece of fluff my roommate left out for me recently, which had eerie echoes of my own life right down to the contra dancing, devoured in one sitting in a sunny kitchen chair. An email arrives in my inbox at a variable time each morning, containing a single poem selected by a man I've never met. Sometimes I smuggle home a collection of short stories or a handful of graphic novels to keep on my bedside table, where academic literature is not supposed to sit (this rule is flexible; I am weak): Ursula K. Le Guin and A.K. Summers; Lucy Knisley and Joey Comeau and Mona Awad, and, and, and... Every once in a while a line catches me sideways, makes me gasp a little and sway. Remembering that I do love the language. Remembering what it's like to breathe deeply.

Kaitlin Heller

Sleeping under the Mountain

> 766 *The Seven Sleepers.* This miscellaneous type comprises various tales dealing with persons who are cast into a magic sleep extending over many years [D1960.1].[1]
>
> > —From Uther's *Types of International Folktales*, based on the system by Antti Aarne and Stith Thompson, which is commonly called the Tale Type Index.

5. Captain America

Ask any of my friends and they'll tell you I love Captain America. I've dressed up as him, I've written stories about him, and I'm known as "Steve" to my closest pals.

---

1 Hans-Jörg Uther, *The Types of International Folktales: A Classification and Bibliography, Based on the System of Antti Aarne and Stith Thompson, Part I: Animal Tales, Tales of Magic, Religious Tales, and Realistic Tales, with an Introduction*, FF Communications 284 (Helsinki: Suomalainen Tiedeakatemia, 2004), 423.

IMAGE: Helping make the bed. PHOTO: Kaitlin Heller.

Steve Rogers was created by Jack Kirby and Joe Simon in 1941 primarily for the purpose of punching Nazis. When the character needed a reboot in the sixties, a sequel story was added in *Avengers* #4: at the end of World War II, Rogers plummeted from a plane into Arctic ice. There he was frozen for years before being thawed and welcomed into both 1960s society and the new Avengers superteam. Much was made of his struggle to fit in; he was dubbed the "Man Out of Time."

There's a great gifset on Tumblr of all the Avengers paired with Disney characters. Cap, of course, is Sleeping Beauty. In the gif, Steve and Aurora bat their eyelashes slowly and synchronously, taking in the world.

Grad school is a lot like being frozen in a block of ice.

At the beginning of my year of comprehensive exams, when I had to read and be examined on approximately two hundred books, I discovered I had practically lost the ability to read. That summer, I sat down to read *A Dance with Dragons*, which was a book I'd waited to read for over a decade, and I couldn't read it. My eyes would slide off the page, I'd get anxious, and I'd have to close the book. When I tried again, I'd realize I hadn't absorbed the previous paragraph, so any ground I gained had slipped out from under me and I had to go backward in order to try to go forward.

The first time this happened, I was lying in Christie Pits, which is a park in Toronto not far from my campus, trying to have a nice day out. I went home and cried. When I had to hit my comps books, it only got worse.

Eventually, I realized that just banging my head against those books wasn't going to get me anywhere. So I developed a system of writing when I read: I would skim as fast as I could, flying over the pages, and take notes as I went. I could do three or four books a day that way, which was good, because by then I didn't have a lot of time left.

I retained that technique for the rest of grad school. It got me through my dissertation. I read in pre-designated chunks, in systems. I built up lists of what I had to read and knocked them down like dominos. Perhaps the taxonomic method matched my environment; Robarts Library, that great concrete turkey, housed the tiny garret designated as my carrel. Brutalism is a great architecture in which to be miserable.

My ability to process information for work was sufficient, though it took an incredible amount out of me. I developed some sort of fatigue in year five that persisted until after I left Canada; when I went to the doctor about it, she said, "It's just grad school." On the truly exhausting days, I would wake up, read and write for an hour, and then need to lie down until evening, when I would make myself dinner. I could read for work, though it seemed to be drawing on my last reserves.

But with a few exceptions, my ability to read for fun didn't recover.

2. *Arthur*

Before I went back to academia, I was an editor. I worked for Del Rey Books, one of the two science fiction and fantasy imprints at Random House; the other is Bantam Spectra, where George R.R. Martin's editor works.

I had come to Random House fresh from my master's degree at Cambridge, during which time I'd given my very first conference paper, about the reception of the Arthurian material in the *History of the Kings of Britain*.

Perhaps because of the confluence of those things, or because I was reading fantasy manuscripts at a truly astonishing rate, or because I was rereading *A Song of Ice and Fire*, this was the first moment I began to see the secret source material on which GRRM had drawn in order to create his epic. (Buy me a drink sometime and I'll tell you what it is. I know I'm right, because I successfully predicted a scene that later appeared in *A Dance with Dragons*.) The point isn't what the source material was. The point was the returning.

Coming back to those books, which had been formative in my teenage years, allowed me to see things I'd never seen before. I contained more stories than I had when I first read the series; now I could find the same story in different places, pick up the same thread.

As I worked at Random House, my ability to read for pleasure outside of work diminished. For a while, I could still read comics; then even that started to fail me. By the time I moved to Toronto for grad school, most of my reading was re-reading.

Many Arthur stories say that he's sleeping in Avalon and will return when Britain needs him.

The critics say there is no king. The king is just a story.

7. *Heller*

In my conception of the world, reading is the opposite of sleep.

A lot of us have this story: when I was a kid, I used to drive my parents crazy with reading. I stayed up until the hours got small and then big again, devouring books whose size made my teachers shake their heads when I carted them around at school. I read my own books and then I read my parents' books. When we visited my grandparents, I read their books too. My parents would snore in the nearby bed while I tossed back and forth on my sleeping mat finishing *The Hound of the Baskervilles*, thrilled and biting my fingernails in terror.

I used to think I wasn't sleeping because I was reading. Now I think I was reading because I wasn't sleeping.

I have a sleep disorder. My various therapists and I aren't sure exactly which one. The best guess I have is delayed sleep phase disorder, which means that I actually sleep the same hours as an average person, but at later times: 2 AM to 12 PM would be ideal, as far as my body's concerned. Labor activist and disability activist friends have introduced me to the radical idea that this disability, like many others, is actually a function of being disabl*ed* by society. The capitalist expectation that we start work at 9 AM is arbitrary but pernicious.

Holding down an office job meant that I was permanently exhausted. I very rarely sleep through *all* my alarms, but you'll notice the plural. My cat is the most effective alarm, a fact of which I believe she is keenly aware.

In grad school, I would work until I passed out at 2 or 3 AM — 4 or later on bad nights. Some of my therapists tried to discourage me from doing this, but by the end of the dissertation I did anything I could to get the work done. Work took the place of reading.

How did I use to read? How could I lose this thing that was so essential to me?

3. *Herla*

Twelfth-century writer Walter Map tells a story about King Herla which was the basis for a different conference paper. I gave the paper at the New Chaucer Society conference in Reyjavík in July; the sun was only dim for a handful of hours at night. By then I was thinking hard about sleep, and travel, and time. Everyone complained about how much the daylight messed with their sleep schedules. I have never in my life slept so well as I did there.

King Herla, if you want to know, went into a mountain for a wedding and came out hundreds of years later. No one knew him; he barely spoke the language. He and his train were cursed never to be able to rest, and so they travel ceaselessly on the earth — or they did, until Map's time, when they were seen plunging into the Wye.

Walter Map told this story because he felt that Herla and his Wild Hunt had passed their cursed restlessness on to his own time. It's hard not to feel his exhaustion, even across the centuries. Sleep is a skipping of time, after all. Sleep is time travel; it connects the past and the present. I think a lot of us understand what it is to wake up in a world that frightens you.

I stopped reading the news a couple years ago. I would wake up in the morning, open a browser, and then I would remember.

There was little left to read after that.

1. Ḥoni HaMe'aggel

I will tell you this story as I understand it from the Talmud.

> One day Ḥoni was out walking and saw a man planting a carob tree. He asked the man when it would bear fruit; the man replied that it would not bear fruit for seventy years. When Ḥoni then asked him if he thought he would live that long, the man said, "Trees now flourish which were planted for me. I plant this one for those who will come after me." Ḥoni laid down to sleep beneath the tree. A cliff or mountain formed around him and he slept under it, hidden from view. He slept so long that when he woke, the tree had borne fruit, and a different man was picking the carobs. That man said that his grandfather had planted the tree for him. "I have slept for seventy years," Ḥoni said to himself. When he went home, no one recognized him. They would not believe that he was Ḥoni. Anguished, Ḥoni asked God for mercy. He died shortly thereafter.[2]

---

2   Talmud, *Ta'anit* 23A, pp. 120–21 of the Steinsaltz Edition (Vol XIV, Part II).

The epigraph at the beginning of this essay is from the new edition of the *Tale Type Index*. It lists the entry for the type known as "The Seven Sleepers." Like all entries in the index, each type is given a heading with the title and summary of the story fitting that type which is, one might say, archetypal; to oversimplify, it is either viewed as the original or the epitome of the tale type. "The Seven Sleepers" is a Christian and Islamic legend. A common medieval Christian form has the eponymous Seven sleeping inside a mountain for hundreds of years and thereby escaping Roman persecution.

Surely this tale type is misnamed. Tale type 766, in its oldest, most archetypal form, is "Ḥoni and the Carob Tree," or perhaps simply "The Carob Tree."

Being a folklorist means returning to the same story over and over. It means being able to see the same story no matter what it's wearing, no matter where you find it. It means reading and rereading, listening and relistening. It means recognizing that even though the tree has grown, it's still the same carob tree.

This is what the translation and commentary in this edition of the Talmud relates at the end of the story:

> Commenting on Ḥoni's death, Rava said: This is what people mean when they say the popular proverb: "Either companionship or death." Man is in great need of companionship. A person who is unable to satisfy that need prefers death to a life of solitude.[3]

Being an academic means spending a lot of time alone. It is a life of solitude.

---

3 Talmud, *Ta'anit* 23A, p. 121.

SLEEPING UNDER THE MOUNTAIN

By the way, Jack Kirby and Joe Simon were Jewish. Cap carries a shield with a big star on it. *Magen* means *shield*. Stan Lee wrote *Avengers* #4, in which Cap sleeps under the ice and wakes up to find that the world is changed. Stan Lee was also Jewish; maybe he knew the story of the carob tree.

... Okay. Maybe not. Maybe it's a coincidence.

Here's what I discovered when I finally started teaching my own classes, after finishing my dissertation. One of them was a class on fairy tales, and I was finding that even though it was hard to read a story or article the first time — grueling, slow, only possible through taking notes — it was somehow easy to read it again.

My students sometimes find it difficult to understand the point of repetition. Why tell the same story different ways? Why tell the same story over again? "For the feeling," said one of my undergraduate professors, the great Deborah Foster. But also because the story changes over time. Even if the words are exactly the same as when you left them, the eyes you read them with are different. The story stayed in place, planted like a tree. You changed around it. You, not the story, are out of time.

4. Sleeping Beauty

Sleeping Beauty gets her own tale type, by the way: 410. But I think when most people think of sleeping for a hundred years, they think of her. She isn't destined to save anyone, like King Arthur or Captain America; she's destined to be saved.

But what makes Sleeping Beauty special, of course, is that she isn't alone. She takes her whole kingdom with her.

After I finished my degree, I decided to try reading my mom's favorite mysteries. I read tons of my mom's collection of mysteries when I was a kid; for a long time, I wanted to be Hercule Poirot. Perhaps I thought I could recapture that magic with this new series. Or perhaps it was because so many of the women I was friends with had been bothering me for years to read them. At any rate: I decided to read the Lord Peter Wimsey mysteries.

It was slow going at first. Sayers was staggeringly sexist, racist, and antisemitic; I nearly quit in the first fifty pages of the first mystery. But after a while those traits faded (mostly), and even at my slow pace, I began to lose myself in her vivid prose and even livelier characters.

It took me nearly two years to read all of them. I read little else in that time; those books travelled with me on a road trip across America, on plane trips, on stalled Amtrak trains. And when I finally read *Gaudy Night*, in which the hero must make important decisions about whether and how to pursue a life of the mind, I suddenly felt behind me a long chain of women reading: my friends; my mother; Sayers herself, who was a medievalist. A whole kingdom. I thought of how we humans repeat these stories, over and over, living them in our various ages.

I thought of how exhausting it is to carry around the expectations of patriarchy when all you want is a good view of Oxford and enough time to finish your book.

Tumblr user soupwife puts it better than I can:

> its tuesday, ive had a glass of wine, and honestly Aurora Knew what the fuck she was doin when she pricked her finger on that spindle man. she was TIRED. she was fully done dude. She was 16 YEARS OLD!!!! if i had the chance to sleep for a hundred years when i was 16 you know id take my chances[4]

6. Aragorn

Enough has been said about Aragorn's parallels with Arthur by others more expert on the subject than I. For the purposes of this essay, this is the important thing about Aragorn, whose mortal sleep does not end: Aragorn is the character for whom the third book in Tolkien's trilogy is named. He is the one who returns in *The Return of the King*, after he passes under the mountain.

Returning, as Tolkien knew, was hard: *how do you pick up the pieces of an old life?*

When I was in college, I took a class on Tolkien with only one prerequisite: that you had read *The Lord of the*

---

4 Soupwife (@soupwife), "its tuesday," Tumblr, May 31, 2016, https://soupwife.tumblr.com/post/145237353596/its-tuesday-ive-had-a-glass-of-wine-and-honestly.

Rings. As of two weeks before class, only two people had failed to meet that requirement — me and the professor.

He, of course, rectified that. But for years, I didn't. I couldn't. I'd tried.

I loved *The Hobbit* when I was a kid. During a long cross-country trip with my dad, I read the whole thing aloud to him while he drove. It's a great book for kids, and it had always been one of my dad's favorites. I had such happy memories of it.

But *The Lord of the Rings* flummoxed me. I couldn't get past the barrow-downs. I just found it exhausting; my eyes would slide off the page, or I'd read the same paragraph twice, and then I'd get frustrated and put it away. The whole time I was an editor at Del Rey Books, I was the only person on staff who'd never read the trilogy.

Finally, during my comps year in grad school, I hit upon a different tactic: I decided to read the whole thing out loud.

I'll be honest and admit that this was originally for the person I was dating, who turned out to be a two-timing good-for-nothing. I recorded myself reading and emailed the digital files. But after I dumped the two-timer, I found that I wanted to keep reading. The words were more interesting spoken than on the page; Tolkien's word choice, though elaborate, was careful. So I emailed a bunch of my friends and family and asked if I could read a chapter each to them.

Reading the rest of that trilogy was one of the most remarkable experiences of my life. It had richness and depth I'd never seen before; it spoke to people in ways I'd never known, and talking to them about it was a gorgeous experience. And I discovered how much I identified with

Aragorn, this wild strange nerd who lost himself in the north but returned when his kingdom needed him.

You already know how the grad school story ends, though. I got worse. I did hold readings at my little basement apartment sometimes, called Milk and Cookies after the group of the same name I used to co-run in college. But my reading life fell away.

I'm not the same person I was before I went into the ice.

I read more slowly now. It's harder to focus, to lose myself in the text; sometimes I can do it on long plane rides or if the book is very good. I'm getting better. I am.

It's all the same story, the story I want to find and tell myself: the king will return. Who I am in relation to that story has changed. I used to think of myself as Aragorn. Now I think the critics were right: there is no king.

There is no king because the king is the shield; the king is the grail. The king is the story.

The story is only sleeping.

The story will return.

caused mass conversions.
it was not allowed to ba...
the downfall of Jewry in S...
Bartolomeo repeated the ol...
murdered a Christian child...
...tion and more mass conversion...
At the beginning of the fourteen...
land of Southern Italy seems to b...
peculiar position of the *neophyte*, Jews ...

...ation of the Jews fro...
English Jewry as well, for Sicily ha...
...two centuries already is...
For the present it suffices to underline...
...ed a letter from Sicily, may be an...
...lines in Jewish social strata. Various a...
...correspond with elements from th...
'higher' cultural circles, though differing prec...
...red nature. Our document testifies to...
...ture in which the role and function of th...
...be located. Is this type of document, one fu...
...lthough even here or maybe precisely here, s...
...m behind conventional forms and norms.

Jennifer Jordan

Reading to Forget, Reading to Remember
Working with Anxiety and Dissociation

Content notes: anxiety, trauma, 9/11, family.

I was nine, and I was meeting my new extended stepfamily for the first time. I shook hands politely but silently as I walked in the door. These pleasantries concluded, I found a seat on the most out-of-the-way, least peopled couch, and retrieved a paperback from a weathered Jansport backpack. Probably R.L. Stine or Christopher Pike, though around that time I was also making my first ventures into Stephen King's body of work. The outside world got quiet, eventually retreating to the peripheries of my attention. The book became my world, as every book did.

Sometime later (thirty minutes? ninety?), more new family members arrived. I failed to notice my new Aunt Dottie's approach, led over by my father who had come to introduce us. "Oh, are *you* the anti-social one?"

I *was* the anti-social one, I knew, but it still hurt. My parents' divorce had been messy, and I was often enlisted

---

I would like to thank my initial readers, Yalile Suriel, Gina Marie Guadagnino, Gil Varod, and my husband, Stephen Danay, for their support of and comments on this piece. Conversations I had over many years with my advisor Sara Lipton, as well as professors Shirley Lim and Jennifer Anderson in the Stony Brook University history department, were also invaluable.

PHOTO: Jennifer Jordan.

to relay messages between hostile parties. Where was the child support check? Did the new hearing date work for everyone? As a result, when not called on as intermediary, I often retreated within myself. Meeting new people made me very nervous — each new acquaintance was potentially someone whose moods and needs I would need to learn to anticipate and accommodate. At home and at school I worried about my parents, about what other people were thinking about me, about how I looked and how people thought I looked, about what I said and whether I had said it correctly. The only thing that silenced these anxious thoughts was reading. I read voraciously — novels, magazines in doctors' waiting rooms, cereal boxes at breakfast, menus and advertisements at restaurants. The words on the page drowned out the incessant inner litany of worst-case scenarios.

Now, after a decade of therapy and quite a bit of research, I understand that I was reading to dissociate. Psychiatrist Judith Herman describes dissociation as the "fragmentation, whereby trauma tears apart a complex system of self-protection that normally functions in an integrated fashion."[1] Reading allowed me to step outside of myself and focus on something that was not my own muddled interiority. In reading dissociatively, I was able to detach from others and from myself. I was creating a kind of double-self: there was the me that thought and felt, and the me that read. I was reading to forget the former.

---

1 Judith Herman, *Trauma and Recovery: The Aftermath of Violence — From Domestic Abuse to Political Terror* (New York: Basic Books, 2015), pp. 34.

— § —

I carried this kind of reading with me to college, and (for the most part) it served me well. Starting my university career at NYU in the fall of 2001 meant that the normal struggles to adjust were amplified by the sudden need to cope with what I had witnessed on September 11th as an eighteen-year-old away from home for the first time. A freshman honors seminar on Abelard and Heloise with the brilliant historian Penelope Johnson provided the material in which I lost myself when I had trouble dealing with my anxieties. It was in this class that I learned the foundations of the skills that would carry me into a graduate career in history; nevertheless, because I engaged with the class material dissociatively, there were aspects of academic life that were difficult for me. I was usually silent, though attentive, in class discussions. If the book was not open in front of me, I struggled to hold onto the specifics of what I had read. I could answer questions about arguments and style but fine details often eluded me.

While reading Suzanne Akbari's thoughts about fast and slow reading in the blog post from which the *How We Read* project was born, I was struck by the degree to which her description of fast reading spoke to the problems I now recognized I faced. For me, dissociative reading was all about speed, "a certain kind of flavor of reading pleasure: a highly superficial, super-fast, super-shallow engagement with language."[2] But Suzanne's fast reading came in tandem with a slower mode of close reading; it was this that

---

2   Kaitlin Heller and Suzanne Akbari, "How We Read," *In the Middle* (blog), October 3, 2017, http://www.inthemedievalmiddle.com/2017/10/how-we-read.html.

I found myself struggling to do in my senior year. I could only read rapidly, and I retained little of what I read. After all, I was reading not to remember, but to forget.

These issues, nascent as I wrapped up my undergraduate career, presented themselves fully when I embarked upon graduate study. A PhD in history seemed like a natural fit for me; it required an abundance of time alone with books. But the reading issues that I had been able to work with while managing an undergraduate workload became unmanageable as I finished my doctoral coursework and began researching my dissertation. I began to worry obsessively about my inability to remember what I read and that I might be regularly missing information that was crucial to my research. Getting through a single page of a monograph or article took far too long, as every sentence was something I needed to remember, something that required I stop and underline or relay into my handwritten notes. With fierceness I tried to hold onto the words on the page, and with relentlessness, they eluded me.

How could I adapt to the reading requirements of advanced research? If what had gotten me through school (and life) to the present moment was dissociative reading, could I move towards a more engaged reading? Perhaps, towards a grounded reading?

— § —

In trauma studies, groundedness is the state opposite to dissociation.[3] If trauma and dissociation are states of

---

[3] For a discussion of grounding and techniques for its cultivation, see Peter A. Levine, *In an Unspoken Voice: How the Body Releases Trauma and Restores Goodness* (Berkeley: North Atlantic Books, 2010), 117–19.

fragmentation, then grounding connotes wholeness, an integration and reconnection. Reading had been my strategy for cultivating a protective, maladaptive dissociation when overwhelmed with anxiety; but academic training required of me a kind of reading where I was engrossed yet present. Over time, I have accrued a number of tactics that have helped me maintain something approaching a grounded mode of reading. To echo sentiments presented in the introduction to this volume's precedent, *How We Write*, this is not a guide to how *to* read, but rather how *I* read — or, how I have come to read after a long process of transition and adjustment. I offer these tips not as universal maxims, but in the hopes that those working on their own mastery of academic reading might find something among the methods I have cobbled together.[4]

One of my pre-requisites for embarking upon difficult reading is meditation, which encourages the meditator to distance herself from her thoughts while still paying attention to them (as opposed to being overwhelmed by them as I often was, or to the dissociative erasure of the thoughts I aimed for as a child).[5] After struggling with a period of burnout after advancing to candidacy, I began to meditate

---

4 In her introduction to the volume, Suzanne states that "there's no single 'right' way to write, and exposure to that range of practices might help those who are in the process of mastering academic writing...most of all by demonstrating that such 'mastery' is an ongoing — potentially limitless — effort." Suzanne Conklin Akbari, "Introduction: Written Chatter and the Writer's Voice," in *How We Write: Thirteen Ways of Looking at a Blank Page*, ed. Suzanne Conklin Akbari (New York: punctum, 2015), xiv.

5 *Nota bene*: Mindfulness meditation can be difficult for those experiencing PTSD. See https://www.headspace.com/blog/2016/12/11/meditating-with-ptsd/ for tips on how to adapt mindfulness practice to accommodate trauma (content note for references to sexual assault).

for five minutes before each reading session. Eventually my initial struggles to quiet the mind gave way to an ability to wield my focus with more precision through persistent non-identification with the thoughts that attempt to hijack that same focus.

Material aids have been just as helpful. Stephanie McKellop, an early Americanist graduate student at the University of Pennsylvania, has tweeted extensively about adapting to graduate school with trauma and its attendant conditions. She frequently recommends plastic reading guides that I have found to be particularly useful in my own reading efforts.[6] Many anxious readers describe a scenario likely familiar to many: when anxious thoughts intrude upon and fragment the attention, one loses their place in the text and ends up reading the same few lines over and over in increasing frustration. These text highlighters, which are made both for reading on screens and "analog" reading, help me to focus my eyes on the text I'm encountering one word at a time. When I use text highlighters I find myself losing my place and re-reading text far less frequently than during unaided reading.

The most significant adjustment, however, has been an ad hoc process of brain-training that has allowed me to trust my ability to remember and process what I read. This strategy has been crucial in helping me to curb the compulsive note-taking that I had adapted to work around my dissociative tendencies. For years, my lengthy and comprehensive notes had served as a breadcrumb trail to lead me back to the page when thrown off track. To break this dependence, I began to make deals with myself: I would stop and take notes only after I had finished a full page

---

[6] Stephanie McKellop, Twitter post, February 12, 2018, https://twitter.com/mckellogs/status/963145918211088384.

of reading, which forced me to rely on recall and meant I was processing what I read rather than simply transcribing. I gradually incremented my reading chunks: first, a page, then two pages, then three. When I had developed sufficient confidence to handle these small segments, I switched over to timed periods: fifteen minutes, then twenty, then thirty. I still struggle with dissociation while reading on occasion, but I try to respond with kindness and accommodation — by incrementing back down the scale and working my way back up — rather than with the cycle of self-reproach and anxious thinking that contributed to the memory issues necessitating this emergency support system in the first place. I remind myself that reading is a skill but also a muscle: the more you do it, the more efficiently it works.

Conclusions have always eluded me. I do not finish many things, to be frank; my particular flavor of perfectionism has meant that for a long time, I expended my energy on beginning things and then, endlessly and compulsively, re-beginning them. The prospect of finishing something would fill me with anxiety, and anxiety would compel me to dissociate, and each return to a project felt like a new start. But a gradual move towards longer and more stable periods of grounding, aided by a shift in how I engaged with texts, has allowed me to approach anxious episodes with more resources and see things through to their ends. The editors of this volume called for academic readers to reflect upon the kinds of reading in which they are engaged. Like many scholars, I was drawn to the academy by a love of reading. However, the reading mode I utilized as an anxious, traumatized child — once essential to survival and now maladaptive and constraining — was inadequate to the demands of advanced graduate study. As the reasons I read changed from personal and dissociative (to escape) to grounded and communal (participating in my graduate work and community), I recognized that I had to change the way I read in order to change the way I process what I read. I cannot read medieval chronicles and sociological theory towards a dissertation chapter the way I once read Stephen King to shut out Aunt Dottie and a new step-family that overwhelmed my senses. By acquiring a skillset that works on a sliding scale, I have been able to incrementally retrain myself to read in a manner more conducive to my academic practice. Adapting my reading process helped me transition from reading to keep the world out to reading to let the world, and the page, in.

Brantley Bryant

Best Practice Tips and Strategies for Academic Reading to Maximize Your Time and Productivity

📖 Highlight words at random. Look for unexpected connections. This can help you remember the text and also create a new text through your reading.

📖 When doing academic reading, first choose your topic of study; for example, an author.
   First, read everything that author wrote.
   Next, read everything that author read.
   Next, read everything the writers that the author read read.
   Next, find the writers read by the writers read by the writers the author read. Read their work as well.
   Congratulations: you are now confident enough to write a short email about some aspect of the topic.

📖 Remember a book from your childhood: *The Eagle of the Ninth*. One evening you were reading while eating a lobster tail. You were reading and eating, happy as the past can make us be, with one of those cups of butter melted to the color of sunshine.

Now, in the past, spill it on the book. Go ahead. Somewhere in the middle. Just make a wave of marigold on that page. Like a savory highlighter pen was broken above it.

When you brought the book to class it smelled like butter and lobster.

📖 You felt the worst about those EETS volumes in the graduate reading room. Poor nineteenth-century Middle English nerdlabor. Bound poorly and printed on paper almost comically unsuited for handling the passage of time. Brittle, cracky, and thin. Every time you brought a book to the photocopier it snowed words on the way. Chits and squares and flakes falling. Pages increasingly unmoored in their binding, wiggling like plants in weak soil. The destruction flying on high in the night. The end of their bookly combination. The path to forgetting.

📖 There is no "I" in "read."

📖 Visualize a goose that just pads through your room, honking, at the exact moment when you pick up the book. It's a solid goose, with brown and white feathers and big, prongy, traffic-cone orange feet. And it's just LOOKING at you. Let me tell you this bird has mean-ass eyes, like it's drilling a hole in your pretensions of *doing* something by reading. Like it *knows* that reading isn't work.

"You think you have it hard?" is what this goose's expression says, "You have no idea."

"Did anyone ever build a bridge by reading a lot?" the goose asks, "Did they?"

- Purchase an array of *Very Short Introductions* to gesture at the topics you feel you owe some delving. These attractively designed volumes are slim, palm-sized. Several of them can be slid into carry-on luggage so that when you are taking a flight or waiting in the airport for hours you can avoid reading them.

- Realize that most likely when you die there's probably a 50/50 chance you'll forget everything you have read.

- Read with earplugs. Read with headphones. Read with an iPod plugged in but no music and nobody says hi. Read with ambient music to smooth out the street noises, the people riotously drunk on the stoop below, the roommate's 3 AM guitar, the people sad yelling, the people happy yelling. Refuse the refusal of the world to render you as alone as you would wish to be so that you finally could read perfectly without leaving a stain or losing an impression.

- Write notes in books to an imagined future reader. Spill your guts. When you lend them to colleagues by mistake this will create some truly wacky moments.

- Keep an omnibus of *The Gormenghast Novels* by the side of your bed. Wait until a spring when you move away from a place you love, then leave the book carelessly in a damp garage for several months. The book will begin to bloom, to mustily inflate as if the pages are spreading bark and fungus. Turning the pages becomes like opening a complicated fruit and there are creaking noises. Return it to the side of your bed.

📖 One of your favorite places to read exists only in your fading memory of a small room in a house knocked down more than ten years ago after the people who lived there all died. That room smelled like sunshine heating wood, a sweet faerie kind of smell.

📖 It can be an effective strategy to make a list of books that you would like to read but are certain that you will, in fact, never, ever read.

This strategy will enable you to realize that the book you are now reading purposefully for a project is the most boring of books.

So many other books out there, but this one, wow: what a stinker.

This will allow you a critical detachment, so that it will not be too difficult to check email or look up the history of those things on the front of ships.

What are they called?

Something like ship-figures?

Were they carved by specialists or kind of an amateur thing by the shipmakers?

Or did that vary by time period?

📖 You will find a variety of truisms on the web to the tune of "If you read X hours per day, in Y days you will be a world expert in the field." It's a best practice to become deeply angry about these statements. Contemplate the ways that reading is unquantifiably more than the violence of knifing the oyster of expertise from the shell of the pages. Instead, look at the opalescent wonder of the shell. Or, even better, visit the oyster alive underwater, in its own territory, where you are vulnerable and estranged. Where the water gets into your pages and you bloom.

📖 That one time a friend read "Diving into the Wreck" out loud and the room was all held breath. Readers roam the world in diving gear, dreaming of the next expedition. We recognize each other from our awkward ways of spending time on the surface.

📖 You do a lot of the work of reading in preparation for others. You do a lot of reading things again. It's important to read everything you assign, every time you assign it. The experience of reading changes, you tell the people you teach, always. You'd be a hypocrite not to note those changes yourself, not to observe the different music of the book when read in a joyous April against that same text skimmed listlessly in a desperate October. One time you don't read *Beowulf* again before teaching because you know this translation so well. Nice job, buddy. You spend the whole class period feeling fragmented, drifting, unsure of what the text in question is. Where is the bright cup? The dragon is fire and forgetfulness; the dragon is despair. The dragon is the last reading.

📖 Just remember that every second you spend asleep is another second you could be re-reading the famous really long Middle English poem *Piers Plowman*.
   Some people really get *Piers Plowman,* but for you it just falls out of your head as soon as you read it.
   Even though *Piers Plowman* specialists are nice, you fear their disregard.

Become so focused on reading *Piers Plowman* and being able to remember every detail afterwards that you read with an exhausting intensity.

This causes you to go to sleep.

The Vision You Have While Sleeping

In a green glade you are going, unglad of your time
Full oft forgetting the facts of Will's far travels
When a goose grim and great gets your attention
That honker heaving heavy human words you-wards:
"Hey buddy, why so perplexed by a book?"

📖 Out of the corner of your eye you think you see the goose's wings spread. Red-gold, covered with scales like armor. You smell soot. But then it's just a goose again, threatening but comical.

📖 Apologize to every book you tote around with you from place to place. You've put them through so much. Ever since that first butter stain! Pen marks. Dog ears, cat ears, tiny folds of mouse ears. Stuffed into boxes, bent, heaved. Awkwardly lurched about. Rings of coffee. Rings of wine. Fine splatters of unruly soups. The terrible arrangements you've accidentally devised. Stacked vertically Babel-high then knocked over at 3 AM. Pressed uncomfortably diagonal on shelves each elbowing the other like the angriest commuters going into the future. You are sorry for them, and also a partner in the honest vulnerability of their materiality.

- 📖 You do a lot of reading for others. Reading as performance, explanation, elaboration. The public and collaborative reading in a group. Piecing through a poem. Asking questions. Reading in tandem. Leading reading. Closing in on close reading. Sometimes you feel vertigo when the dragon weaves in and out of a moment, reminding all present of their contingency.

- 📖 Remember back to how sublimely organized you were in graduate school. You photocopied whole volumes. You sat at that one cheap walnut desk in the room with the air conditioner and you would type out whole passages word for word, making reading into data entry. A couple years later downloading PDFs became easier. They bought a fast scanner at work. Now you make notes in pen on the texts themselves and keep copies of your own scribblings. You are a diligent self-publisher.

- 📖 You may have the good fortune to know people who write books. Eventually, your slow and sporadic reading will become not only an intellectual failing but a failure to properly appreciate the work of your friends. Read faster!

- 📖 Try to recall the plot of a novel you read several years ago every night on a family trip to Disneyland. Write down four key details and see if they match the description of the book you find online. Consider checking in with friends about the duration of their novel-reading memories. How well can they remember the plot, characters, and important passages of books read only once, for fun, after a bright day, to the sound of someone snoring, in a small hotel with plastic icicles in June?

📖 You didn't read "real books" when you were younger. You read fake books before anything. Fake books you read and to fake books you shall return. D&D rulebooks. Comprehensive episode annotations for *Star Trek*. Overwrought vampires traveling in France. Oh, the high school teachers shook their heads and tried to get you to read something else. Where was the real thing? You chose the books with dragons.

📖 Research shows that scholarly best practice is to read as an extended penance, an apology for even taking on a topic in the first place. Start with recent articles related to the topic, then recent articles tangentially related to the topic. Then suggestions. It is a dialogue with other scholars, but the kind of dialogue that occurs when you enter a gymnasium crowded with people smarter than you and you stand off to the side, clearing your throat. Eventually you scribble a note to someone and they take the note without looking at you and they continue to talk.

📖 There are those who swallow scholarly books. They devour journal issues. They down a whole festschrift like a piece of sushi, chewing awkwardly but getting the job done so fast. To you devourers — cheers! You are magicians and wonders. But you others, you who are easily distracted, you know the feeling. That you are reading this now is amazing. Perhaps take a moment to finally read that piece you have on an open tab in your browser. The goose will watch.

📖 "You think you know so much about dragons," says the goose, "but you've got them wrong. You think you have lived long with them, but your time has been so short.

The sum of what we destroy is nothing compared to the amount of riches that we guard. We hoard for you. We make sure the past won't shift out from under us. The dragon is the center of the map."

📖 What is the first "complicated" book you read? Was it *Dune*? Simple maybe now, but it had heft and a glossary in the back. You read it in a place where you could see the ocean. Pretended the beach sand was Arrakis. Transported into fantasies of heroes.

📖 Read, if nothing else, in alliance with all readers. In alliance with readers whose engagements have been deeply different. In alliance with readers who do not see themselves here. A proposal that reading is as singular as a life or a love affair. A proposal that one "how" of "we read" is how to read together so that none of us is forgotten. We the singular. We the together-estranged. We have all sensed wings.

📖 A quiz. Academic reading, for you, is:

    A) A substitute for a passion you once lost.
    B) A means to an end.
    C) The thing itself.
    D) A means to delay the inevitable.
    E) You need time to research your answer.

📖 Sometimes reading is an excuse for sitting on the carpet with the rain in the window and and the cat sitting by your shoulder. You are concerned about the cat's new awkward walk, a sign of age. Cancel more plans.

📖 You have permission to leave a food or drink stain on this book, right here on this side of the page. Choose something good. Make sure to do this before you move to the next (and last) piece of advice below.

※ PLEASE STAIN BELOW THE DOTTED LINE. ※

....

📖 "Buddy!" Oh damn it's the middle of the night and pressing on your chest is a heaviness like a heart attack and you're wide awake. The goose is waddling right on top of you, thumping down its heavy feet. It smells like mud. "Buddy! Buddy!" The bird is in your face. "Buddy! Remember when you read *The Hobbit* and you never wanted to leave? You set up a tent in the back yard, when your family lived on that base. One of those old lanterns." This is awkward, and rushed, and the goose clearly has tragically wrong ideas about how to use personal space. But the goose has a point. Reaching back to that memory, you feel sustained in a moment of many troubles and worries and awarenesses of failings. You feel an absolutely pure love. Something that can never fade or be taken away. Not as long as you are here. The goose's face is next to yours, turned for one eye to stare right at you and you see that its eye is not a regular goose eye but a kind of ridged canyon of a great serpent's eye, eerie moonscape of a wyrm's eye looking out from something ancient and wonderful and terrible. "That was reading, that time we first met," says the goose, "that was reading."

Kaitlin Heller

Afterword
The Parlor Scene

At the end of a classic mystery, the famed detective gathers all the key players into a room and reveals the solution. Order is restored; the puzzle box is closed; what was invisible is revealed. Each turn of the story settles, to the reader's satisfaction, into its proper habitation and name. That elegant taxonomy pervades this book.

When I first gathered all these essays to read them together, sitting on a muddy lawn in front of the Hall of Languages at Syracuse University, I noticed that many of us shared a library. Lochin's spreadsheet of the works of Agatha Christie rubbed elbows with Kirsty's loaned copy of *The Nine Tailors*. The copies of *Encyclopedia Brown* that Chris read twice, because he liked knowing the answer, jostled Anna's well-labeled fanfiction, her collections of murder mysteries, and her beloved genre fiction. Although they are not, strictly speaking, mysteries, Jessica's Choose Your Own Adventure books keep company here: just as Lochin deconstructed, labelled, and epitomized the laws of the mystery genre, so Jessica kept her fingers in the pages of each paperback to retrace the consequences of each choice.

This does not seem to me to be a coincidence. Rather, it is a telling clue about how we read, and why: these are readers of mysteries in more ways than one. Chris pored

IMAGE: After class, Syracuse University, NY. PHOTO: Kaitlin Heller.

over "catalogues of manuscripts, which, in the right hands, could be read like an Agatha Christie." The archivist must be a detective, and must enjoy a good mystery. Yet, too, the historian has the advantage of the detective; "the reader of history," Lochin reminds us, "is a reader who knows how the story ends." The puzzle box is already closed. As Anna notes, in medieval literature, "Everything that can happen to them has already happened." We can open it; we can rearrange it; we can furnish a reader with our own parlor scene from a place outside the mystery.

Genre is powerful. I laughed at Anna's assertion that she doesn't read anything without dragons or spaceships, but I cried when I understood what Brantley's dragon was trying to say: when we stop recognizing the dragon, we have to get to know it again. Being familiar with the dragon, with the tropes, with the genre, is what gives us stability as readers. Our friend the dragon is as reliable and comforting as the detective's puzzle box.

And, too, familiarity gives us access. I was struck by the intimacies of these essays — how these readers see themselves in these stories, as Irina saw herself in Aldhelm's athletes and Lochin saw herself in a saint's life. At times, the only way to access a text might be to localize it in the body. Just as Irina walked out the rhythm of a poem along the water's edge, accessing the text through her stride, and Suzanne read her texts aloud, Lexi disappeared into the text, using her voice to give others access. The tension between presence and absence is felt in the body and the text simultaneously; the body and the text together negotiate a space.

Jenn's struggle to be present in that space highlights the power and the danger of disappearing into a text, and equally, the power of grounding oneself in the world. Her work of acceptance, explicit and organized, seems close kin to Kirsty's meditation on space: the kitchen chair; the bedside table; the itch of reading, even at breakfast. Each visit to the text becomes a distinct departure, and there is always a return to the body afterward.

And the physical sound itself of reading is powerful, both a potential form of access and, as Jonathan notes, a potential form of intimacy, of encounter. The act of reading creates intimacies not only between bodies, but across time: Jonathan's scholarly approach to Margery Kempe and her modalities of reading is inextricable from the physical experiences they share. Stephanie's joy at finding kinship with Reformation annotators and readers, who themselves read aloud and scribbled notes as they went, shapes both her research and her pedagogy. Our connection to the past through our own modes of reading is not trivial; as I said in my own essay, I often find myself returning there.

I wrote this afterword, as I did much of my dissertation, on a Skype call with Jessica Hammer. I think often of what she has taught me about returning — to text, to life, to problems unsolved. We thirten essayists are readers who return. As academics, most of us historians, we've already read the end of the book of time, and we spend a lot of time reading it again, solving the mystery, knowing what will happen.

If you read this essay first instead of last, I hope you had a good laugh about knowing what happens in this book. And if you read it last instead of first, I hope it proved a satisfying ending to the mystery. I also hope that in your life you will not, like me, need quite so long to finish reading your particular dragon. But if you do, rest safe in the knowledge that we understand how you read.

www.ingramcontent.com/pod-product-compliance
Lightning Source LLC
Chambersburg PA
CBHW072045160426
43197CB00014B/2631